CLNW

We hope you enjoy
renew it by the due

You can renew it at w ...norfolk.gov.uk/libraries or
by using our free library app.

Otherwise you can phone 0344 800 8020 -
please have your library card and PIN ready.

You can sign up for email reminders too.

27. JUL. 22

NORFOLK ITEM

30129 084 882 019

NORFOLK COUNTY COUNCIL
LIBRARY AND INFORMATION SERVICE

Also by James Meek

NOVELS
McFarlane Boils the Sea
Drivetime
The People's Act of Love
We Are Now Beginning Our Descent
The Heart Broke In
To Calais, In Ordinary Time

SHORT STORIES
Last Orders and Other Stories
The Museum of Doubt

NON-FICTION
Private Island: Why Britain Now Belongs to Someone Else

DREAMS OF LEAVING AND REMAINING

Fragments of a Nation

James Meek

VERSO
London • New York

This paperback edition first published by Verso 2021
First published by Verso 2019, 2021
© James Meek 2019, 2021
Earlier versions of the following chapters originally appeared in the
London Review of Books: Chapter 1 in vol. 37, no. 8; Chapter 2 in vol.
38, no. 12; Chapter 3 in vol. 40, no. 7; Chapter 4 in vol. 39, no. 8.
Parts of the introduction were recorded as a talk for BBC radio.

1 3 5 7 9 10 8 6 4 2

Verso
UK: 6 Meard Street, London W1F 0EG
US: 20 Jay Street, Suite 1010, Brooklyn, NY 11201
versobooks.com

Verso is the imprint of New Left Books

ISBN-13: 978-1-78873-775-3
ISBN-13: 978-1-78873-525-4 (US EBK)
ISBN-13: 978-1-78873-524-7 (UK EBK)

British Library Cataloguing in Publication Data
A catalogue record for this book is available from the British Library

The Library of Congress Has Cataloged the Hardback Edition as Follows:
Names: Meek, James, 1962– author.
Title: Dreams of leaving and remaining / James Meek.
Description: London ; Brooklyn, NY : Verso, 2019.
Identifiers: LCCN 2018059042| ISBN 9781788735230 (hardback) | ISBN
   9781788735254 (US ebook) | ISBN 9781788735247 (UK ebook)
Subjects: LCSH: European Union – Great Britain. | Great Britain – Economic
   conditions – 1997– | Great Britain – Social conditions – 21st century. |
   Great Britain – Politics and government – 2007-
Classification: LCC HC240.25.G7 M44 2019 | DDC 341.242/20941 – dc23
LC record available at https://lccn.loc.gov/2018059042

Typeset in Adobe Garamond Pro by Hewer Text UK Ltd, Edinburgh
Printed and bound by CPI Group (UK) Ltd, Croydon, CR0 4YY

Their mental state is that of a collectively excited group ruled by affective judgments and wish-fantasies. In a state of 'collective possession' they are the adapted ones and consequently they feel quite at home in it.

Carl Jung, *The Undiscovered Self*

The Spitfire is an iconic symbol of world-class aerospace engineering, and I'm delighted to see this unique piece of British history brought to a global audience.

Liam Fox, Britain's international trade secretary, explaining in 2018 how his government would encourage foreigners to buy British goods by sponsoring a round-the-world trip by an obsolete machine designed to kill foreigners

Contents

Introduction: A Divided Home

As I write this, under the cold white sky of October in London, the ether is filled with maps showing darkness in the North of England, lighter colours in the South. The maps of coronavirus infection seem to reinforce the cliché of an old economic divide – the grim North, with bad diets, overcrowded houses and factory jobs; the rich South, with healthier lifestyles and airy home offices. Earlier in the pandemic, when it was the South that had more cases, the infection was parsed as a different divide, somehow miraculously preserving the same poles of negativity and positivity: the globetrotting pleasure-seekers of the South, who brought home the virus from their travels, contrasted with the less cosmopolitan Northerners.

We've heard the North–South coronavirus divide as the powerful South versus the powerless North – the entire country wrenched around to face whatever way suits London. We've heard it as plaguey cities versus virus-free villages, as refugee second-homers versus holiday area locals, as the young versus the old, as stern Scotland against gadfly England. We've heard it as anti-lockdown libertarians against pro-lockdown communitarians. All this division, when this was supposed to be a country already cloven by Brexit.

'Britain is a divided country' is a safe sort of opinion. But it's a more mysterious proposition than most clichés. It's spoken as if a divided Britain were a bad thing. But consider the opposite.

Statements like 'Britain is a harmonious country' or 'Britain speaks with one voice' carry the tinny squeak of totalitarian propaganda. Free countries are never united. The test of a healthy democracy is its power to air disagreements in the open and settle them without falling back to warlords and armed tribes. Why, then, is the phrase 'Britain is a divided country' pronounced so gloomily? Because it doesn't mean what it seems to mean. It doesn't mean 'Britain is a divided democratic society.' It means 'Britain is a divided home.'

A divided home is more painful than a divided country. There are angry silences, sullen looks, slammed doors, shouting, things broken. There is a sense among some members of the household that other members have lost their minds and they're trapped together, the feeling someone is bringing home the wrong kind of people. How do you react? Perhaps by trying to enforce your will at home over those you think are wrong. Or perhaps by resigning yourself to the fact that being fixed to one place and to one way of living is not the definition of home. Home is where you live. But home is also something you move. Home is something you leave and come back to. And home is something you make. The subtlety of the phrase 'Britain is a divided home' is that it points both to the problem and the cause. Britain is a country split between those who believe the beginning and end of home coincides exactly with the geographical edge of the United Kingdom, and those whose idea of home is something much less certain.

Where does home begin and end? When does being 'away' shift to being 'home'? Is the boundary your own front door? Is it the garden gate or the entrance to your block of flats? Is it when you turn the corner into the street where you live, or is it when you see the landmark that says you've reached your neighbourhood? Is it when the train pulls into your hometown station, or is it when the border official at the airport waves you through with the words 'Welcome back'? Is it when the hatch of your lander opens and you smell sweet terrestrial air and know that, after a long time in space, you're back on Earth?

People who leave the planet experience something called the Overview Effect, a visceral sense of kinship with humanity inspired by witnessing the globe from a distance. After a long stint on the International Space Station the Canadian astronaut Chris Hadfield described the epiphany of seeing Earth as a single home, not in the abstract, but before his eyes, turning by itself in the void. 'Somewhere along the way, in one of those thousands of orbits,' he said, '… you start to see the world as what it actually is … this whole thing is just our collective, shared room.'

For the time being, if we identify ourselves as natives of Earth, there's no other possible home to set against it. When we identify as a native Briton, we set aside the local enmities that divide communities, classes, ethnicities and generations within our home country. We embrace the idea that we share a common national home. But in doing so, we set our home against the national homes of others.

Once, when I worked as a newspaper reporter, a colleague and I found ourselves driving around the Kuwaiti desert in a hired car, trying to tag along with the American and British armies invading Iraq. We accidentally drove into a British military position close to the border that had just been hit by an incoming shell. The troops were jumpy. We found ourselves facing the muzzle of a British soldier's gun. He was crouched in a foxhole in full battle gear and didn't seem inclined to give us the benefit of the doubt.

We stopped and I got out, and a young lieutenant came over to establish our bona fides, stopping to order the soldier, 'Cover me!' in a way that didn't seem trusting. We offered him a copy of a British newspaper we had with us, and what doubts he still had about our identity vanished. 'That's my favourite paper!' he said.

There was a lot of natural tension in that encounter, even after it was established that it wasn't necessary to kill us: tension between the civilian and the military and between people doing conflicting jobs. Still, just for that moment, once the ice was broken, there was what Robert Louis Stevenson calls 'a ready-made affection' – Britons in adversity together, far from their common home.

It was nice; but it was also horrible. That affirmation of a common British home was made at least partly in a spirit of violence against another home, Iraq, which that officer was about to take part in invading, and I, through our brief comradeship, was, if not endorsing the invasion, certainly accepting its inevitability. Some people still believe Britain was right to help America invade Iraq. But even those who don't tend to think of the invasion in terms of national homes: our home should have left their home alone. It's hard for us, in our hearts, to make the astronaut's conceptual jump to seeing all wars as domestic violence.

I've had a long succession of homes. I was born in southeast London and moved when I was three to Nottingham, and when I was five to Polmont near Falkirk, and when I was six to Lanarkshire, and when I was seven to Dundee, and when I was seventeen to Edinburgh, and when I was twenty-one to north London, and when I was twenty-two to Northampton, and when I was twenty-five to Edinburgh again, and when I was twenty-eight to Kiev, and when I was thirty-one to Moscow, and when I was thirty-seven to west London, and when I was thirty-eight to north London, and when I was forty-three to east London, and when I was fifty-three to Norwich, and when I was fifty-six to east London again, and now I'm fifty-seven I live in south-east London, only four miles from where I was born, as if I'd hardly been anywhere.

But home has to be more than a list of dozens of addresses in multiple countries. What about community? Home has a way of spilling over the doorstep. As a small child living in a council house in Nottingham in the 1960s, I used to wander freely into the neighbours' kitchen as if it were my own, to listen to their radio and to have sips of Newcastle Brown Ale offered by the master of the house, sitting like a king at the head of the table in his white vest. And then we moved; work took my father north.

Did home move with us to each new house, to each new town? Or was home frozen at some point along the way? Should I pick Dundee, the city where I lived longest as a child, where I mostly went to school and where my parents still live, as my home, when I haven't lived there for forty years? And is it up to me anyway? I can pick Dundee, but what does Dundee think about it?

Much of the reporting of tension in Britain between so-called local people and migrants evokes an idea of settled communities of natives against foreign incomers. But most migrants in Britain were born in other parts of Britain. If a generation ago people lived, on average, five miles away from where they were born, today the average is a hundred miles. The strength of the modern attachment to the idea of the nation as home may be because the borders of the nation are stable and capacious enough to mask origin anxiety; it's easier to feel at home in Britain when you're not sure whether you're at home in, say, Cornwall, where you were born, or Yorkshire, where you live.

Stability of borders has not been my personal experience. It seems difficult now to define myself as British; I feel under pressure to choose Scotland or England as my home, not both. When I arrived in the other two countries I've lived in, they were parts of the Soviet Union. Now, as Russia and Ukraine, they're at war.

There's another way to determine home, and that's to seek it in time, in family and ancestry, in the murky concept of blood. As a child I divided myself up mentally into different flavoured portions, like a three-cheese pizza, according to my understanding of my parents' nationality: half Scottish, quarter English and quarter Hungarian. I felt sorry for people who only had one flavour. I was proud of my Scottishness among the English, awkward about my Englishness among the Scots, code-switched my accents and, never having been to Hungary and not speaking a word of Hungarian but knowing the culture only through my grandmother's voice and cooking, brought my Hungarianness out on special occasions, like a strange heirloom whose meaning I barely understood but liked to show to friends.

Later, I realised it was more complicated to trace the routes to home through family origins. My father, from whom I thought I derived my Scottishness, was born in India and didn't see the British Isles until he was eight. His father was a second-generation Scottish immigrant to London. My Hungarian grandmother also turned out to be my Jewish grandmother, meaning I would probably find it easier to become a citizen of Israel than a citizen of Hungary. As a mongrel child of the imperial Scottish and Jewish diasporas, with a bit of English arts and crafts thrown in, I feel comfortable in London and comfortable raising a child here. I appreciate the protection of the National Health Service and the rule of law in Britain and would feel their absence in many other parts of the world, and I do like the place. I feel at home in Britain, but that's not quite the same as being sure it is home, even though I was born here, have lived mostly here, have no other passport, have no plans to leave the archipelago and expect to end my days here.

I can see why the idea of Britain as a divided home is more frightening than the idea of Britain as a divided nation. The divided home is an image of discord and mistrust, of family strife and cheating. But it is also an image of freedom and the dynamism of life: in one room, a mother is nursing her child; in another, a young woman is preparing for the exams that will enable her to leave home and make a new one elsewhere; in another, an old man is fading away. Elsewhere in the house, a young man plays music too loudly. In the attic room is a guest who's been there for so long it's almost as if he's part of the family. But you never know. He might leave tomorrow. No-one can say this is not a home, nor can anyone say it isn't changing from one day to the next into something entirely different.

In modern life, very few remain at home forever. Everyone leaves eventually, if only to go to school or to work. In modern life, 'leaving and remaining' actually means 'leaving home, then remaining in the place you went away to, or coming back'. The text of the Brexit referendum read, 'Should the United Kingdom remain a member of the European Union or leave the European Union?' which translates as 'Should I remain away, in the place I left home for, or should I leave the place I went to and go home?' In the distant past, when Britain was a predominantly rural society, the leaving home and the remaining away or leaving to come back again was a momentous affair.

To map that onto modern times we have to turn to neighbour cultures' books like Edna O'Brien's Irish trilogy *The Country Girls*, where young Cait loses her beloved mother, leaves the family farm to go to convent school, then moves to the big city. The farm and the country village are Cait's childhood, her mother, her origin, the wellspring of sensation, intimate and knowable; they are also the imprisoning horror of ignorance, small-mindedness, suffocating religion and her loathsome father. The city is excitement, growing-up, new ideas, limitless possibilities; it is also snobbishness, indifference, alienation, exploitation.

When we talk about such personal versions of leaving and remaining, we tend to use the language of cause, action and decision. 'I decided to move to Liverpool.' 'I had to get away from London.' 'I went to university.' 'After college I moved back home.' 'I've never felt the need to travel outside Norfolk.' What this kind of discourse misses is the hinterland of representation that forms the medium of our psychic lives. We live out our days in action and sensation, but this is embedded in our mental representations of where we've been and where we're going: a mixture of myth, memory and imagination, entwining personal, family and folk-experience that, as well as characterising for us the society that is our home, tells us how that home falls short of what we suppose to be perfection.

The essays collected here, which originally appeared in the *London Review of Books*, are not a psychiatric examination of these representations. But as well as digging into history, looking at the stats and talking to specialists, researching them involved long hours encouraging people who aren't academics or media-habituated experts to tell me about their lives and about the way they see the world at a level of analysis they wouldn't usually have reason to express.

The questions I set out to answer were concrete – why was the United Kingdom Independence Party, initially perceived as a de facto breakaway wing of the Conservatives, so strong in run-down Northern Labour strongholds like Grimsby? What will happen to the countryside if Britain leaves the EU? Is the NHS failing and, if so, why? Are there winners and losers at the two ends of a globalisation chain, or only winners, or only losers? But at the same time I was listening out for something more elusive and intangible – not just what the English 'feel' or 'know' or 'believe' about this or that event, but the fabric of past, present and future within which the

English situate events. There are realms of non-academic, non-journalistic representation of the wider world where the actual, the legendary, the remembered, the anticipated, the heard-about and read-about, the personal and the communal combine to form a framework that both provides the site for and explains events. It is a kind of practical dream.

By 'dream' I don't mean the mental manifestations of sleep or the word's modern sense of 'perfect outcome'. I mean an underlying model of the world, in the sense of the Australian Aboriginal dreaming, a transcendental map-narrative. 'White man got no dreaming,' says the unnamed Aboriginal thinker in W. E. H. Stanner's famous essay 'The Dreaming', but the observation is too absolute.

Just as, in Stanner's account, the Aboriginals he knew could be as logical and rational as any European, even while they lived within the dreaming, so the mental framework of rationality, or common sense, within which the English like to believe they live coexists with a less reasoned world view not so utterly different from the dreaming Stanner describes:

> Although, as I have said, The Dreaming conjures up the notion of a sacred, heroic time of the indefinitely remote past, such a time is also, in a sense, still part of the present. One cannot 'fix' The Dreaming in time: it was, and is, everywhen. We should be very wrong to read into it the idea of a Golden Age, or a Garden of Eden, though it was an Age of Heroes, when the ancestors did marvellous things that men can no longer do.

An inability to articulate the dreaming of the Leavers in full doesn't mean it isn't there. It's about personal ancestors, the things they did and where they came from; it's about remote, titanic figures, some real, some fictional, some generic, a pagan pantheon apart from God – the Queen, Elvis, Churchill, Hitler, James Bond, Sid Vicious, Thatcher, Bobby Moore, the miner, the Spitfire pilot, the NHS nurse – and sacred spaces, some famous, like Wembley or Waterloo or Dunkirk, some idealised, like the factory, the village, the rural military airfield in 1941.

Before the pandemic intruded, each summer in England saw millions of people attending arts and music festivals and sporting fixtures, a rich and familiar cultural calendar well covered in the national media. But each summer, too, invisible to the patrons of Glastonbury and Edinburgh, a similar number of people fought their way through traffic jams and crush barrier–festooned railway stations to attend air shows, a ritual celebration of speed, noise, precision engineering and war – a more mysterious pilgrimage. A typical tour calendar of the Royal Air Force's Red Arrows display team, whose nine aircraft trailing coloured smoke as they perform aerobatics form the highlight of these displays, is dotted with the names of Leave strongholds: Torbay, Great Yarmouth, Cleethorpes, Hastings, Folkestone, Sunderland, Clacton.

In my travels in England, listening to people talk about their lives, I spoke mainly to people in favour of leaving the European Union, since they were the disruptors. I heard many true stories and many strong opinions, but as the years went by I began to attend more and more to the hints of dreaming between the lines, in what was not said as well as what was said. I noticed three things.

One was a strong sense of oppression, of being censored, and an attendant resentment. There were several occasions when Leavers I spoke to left pregnant gaps that could only have been filled with anti-immigrant sentiments that they weren't 'allowed' to say. By no means are all Leavers racist, but I ended up with the impression that, for many, casual racism is regarded as a lost patrimony; that as much as Leavers might oppose immigration, they are no less resentful of the 'elites' rendering it awkward to categorize people along racial lines.

Another thing I noticed was the internationalism of Leavers – internationalism with a particular flavour. The nostalgia for Ian Smith's Rhodesia from a Norfolk farmer and UKIP member of the European Parliament; the desire to roam the North Sea freely without engaging with other littoral countries among Grimsby fishermen; the indignation, from an ex-chocolate factory worker and UKIP member in the west country, that young Britons who want to study abroad 'have to' go to Europe (they don't, but let that pass) when they should be going to Australian universities instead.

The third thing was a preoccupation with the state as defender of its people. This was literal – UKIP fliers boasting of how many extra aircraft carriers they would build once in government – but also figurative: that it was the British government's job to defend native Britons against foreign immigrants, foreign competition, greedy capitalists and, through the National Health Service, illness.

I used to be sceptical of the idea that Britain hadn't come to terms with the loss of its empire. It was such a long time ago, and not one of the many Leavers I've had hours of conversations with over the years has said explicitly that they want it back – how could you?

But I believe now that a subliminal empire does persist in the dreaming of a large number of Britons, hinted at in a longing for the return of guilt-free racial categorization; in the idea that my country can be both globally open and privileged in an international trading system where it can somehow turn the rules to its advantage; in the idea of a safe white core protected from the dark hordes beyond by a mighty armed force.

This is my inheritance too, whether I like it or not, though, as it happens, I don't. We all have to make a psychic home in some sort of shared dream-empire. The world did not begin on the day we were born. The way we represent society to ourselves is not only a representation of how society is but of how it was. It strikes me as I look back over these essays that the people I spoke with were in a constant dialogue with history, consciously or unconsciously, with personal ghosts and with the settlements of historical events: wars, strikes, the births and deaths of industry, the establishment and end of colonies.

Everyone knows how the division of an inheritance can damage those who have a stake in a shared home, but this can take different forms. If the legacy is a shared national dreaming, a common representation of what Britain was and what it became, the point of tension is not so much 'Who gets what?' as 'What do you mean, you don't want it?' Not so much 'This is for you, and this is for me' as 'You never liked it here, you got out as soon as I could,' and 'Is it any wonder I wanted to get out of this dump and make something better of myself?' Not so much 'The picture's ugly, but I'll keep it, it reminds me of Dad,' more 'I know he did some terrible things, but he was our father, and I loved him.'

The second decade of the twenty-first century saw some startling changes in Britain; we saw them happening around us. But it is clear that as the present was changing, the past as we perceived it – our representation of the Britain we had inherited – was changing, too. Those who dreamed the empire, safe at home behind the sea walls of a green and white island fortress tied by great silver planes to other green and white fortresses across the Atlantic and Pacific, are woken by the sounds of screams and falling statues as others who share this home find the empire dream to have always been a nightmare.

London, October 2020

Leaving the Sea and Remaining

Grimsby 2015

In Grimsby, the former fishing capital of England, I saw turnstones scurry across the tarmac of derelict streets. The turnstone isn't a creature of asphalt and paving. It's a small white-breasted bird usually to be found foraging on British foreshores in groups of a score or so, scuttling in sync up and down sandy beaches as the foaming forward edge of the sea roars in and hisses back. It was March 2015, two months before the general election. A prediction that the winner of that election would cause Britain to leave the EU only four years later would have sounded fanciful, but the noisiest supporters of exit were gaining ground. I was in Grimsby to see why, after seventy years of voting Labour, the town was flirting with the United Kingdom Independence Party. After a while I wondered what had happened to make central Grimsby a wild and lonely enough place for the turnstones to roam undisturbed. It turned out the reason was the same.

Some one, or some thing, abdicated power in Grimsby, leaving swathes of it to rot. But who, or what? And what would the succession be?

People tell you in Grimsby that there was only one power. Fish was king, and it didn't abdicate, it was overthrown by foreigners. Once, the world's largest ice factory would turn out gargantuan ice blocks to be crushed by the ton, carried on conveyors to the dockside and poured from chutes into the holds of the world's largest fishing fleet, queuing up for the means to chill their catch before heading for northern waters. When the ships came back they'd bury the quayside in haddock and cod. There were six hundred trawlers in Grimsby in the boom years of the mid-twentieth century, and each good-sized deep sea vessel had twenty men on board. Each man at sea supported four jobs on land. The fishermen were paid a share of the profits made from each three-week trip; after a three-day break they went to sea again, a rhythm that sent pulses of cash-rich fishermen racing to the fleshpots and trinketries of Freeman Street, the backbone of the Victorian town, which ran from the docks to the Marsh districts where the fishermen lived. They would walk away from the cashier at the docks, get into a cab and let the meter run through all their sprees and benders and gift-giving, till the taxi dropped them back off on the quay, quite possibly broke, ready to set sail again.

That was until the 1970s, when Iceland closed its fishing grounds to the British, and European politicians mutualised Europe's seas, including those Britain laid claim to, and told the Grimsby fishermen there weren't enough fish left. They could only catch what Brussels allowed, and when. Boat by boat the fishing fleet was scrapped. Freeman Street darkened.

It is still a desolate place. Half its shops are shuttered. An entire shopping centre lies abandoned. Life expectancy for people born in East Marsh is ten years lower than in the rest of town. The area is at high risk of flooding, and was almost inundated in the storm surge of 2013. Six 1960s tower blocks, each with more than a hundred flats, rise over East Marsh, hard by Freeman Street. Shoreline, the housing association that took over Grimsby's council houses in 2005, intended to knock them down. It wouldn't replace them.

The ice factory was still standing, its machinery intact, but the conveyors were rusting, and although English Heritage had given the vast red brick building a Grade II listing, this hadn't prevented the roof falling in. Since the ice factory roof dominated the skyline, the visitor got the impression the docks had been freshly bombed.

Billy Hardie was there at the end of fishing, a veteran of the Cod War and the glory days before. He was a trawler skipper then – he still captained a boat, now doing survey work – and he'd done well out of it, with a large, comfortable house in the suburbs. His wife had crowded fishing mementoes out of their living room with an abundance of Japonaiserie, and Hardie had to dig down into a stash hidden behind a sofa to show me the trophy he won in 1975. 'Top 139-foot Trawler', the plate read, with the value of the catch engraved down to the last pound: £311,666. As the skipper, Hardie got five per cent, minus five per cent of the cost of the trip – a haul, for three weeks' work, of perhaps £100,000 in today's money.

Hardie, who was seventy-two, had joined Ukip. He'd voted Labour, Conservative and Ukip in the past, but it would be Nigel Farage's party for him this time. For Hardie, it wasn't about immigration – there aren't many immigrants in Grimsby – but about the European Union, and a lingering bitterness over the end of the old fishing days, and a sense that Labour had failed. 'I don't want to be ruled by Europe,' he said. 'Told what I can catch, what I can't catch . . . Why Labour's taken such a big knocking for Grimsby is, why would you vote for them? Take a look at it. What's Labour done for Grimsby? All the industry has gone, we've got vast unemployment. Give somebody else a chance. Labour will lose this seat.'

As a boy growing up in the 1950s Hardie shared a house with his fisherman father and his fisherman grandfather. He lived on the top floor. 'I got up in the morning and could watch the ships going up and down. When I was twelve or thirteen they were saying: "What's young Billy going to do when he leaves school?" He wasn't going to be a plumber. He was going to sea, wasn't he?'

It wasn't an easy way to make a living. Crews worked twelve hours on, twelve hours off while they fared to and from the Icelandic fishing grounds. Once the fishing began, shifts went up to eighteen hours. Between voyages you could take a week off but then the ship would leave without you and someone else would take your place. 'We used to say in fishing the trawler owners were the last of the big Victorian gaffers,' Hardie said. 'Whatever happened, the ship was going back.'

The crews were dogged by superstitious prohibitions. No woman was let on board, and the colour green was taboo, as was any mention or depiction of pigs, or rabbits. The taboos were commensurate with the danger. Hardie's other grandfather died in a U-boat attack in 1939. In 1998 Hardie lost a boat in a freak sea, though he and his crew were rescued. Off Iceland one winter he saw a ship, top-heavy with frozen seawater, capsize with twenty men on board. Only one man survived, his life raft driven into a fjord where, by extraordinary luck, he stumbled across a sheep shed. The warmth of the animals kept him alive until he was rescued.

In the mid-1970s Hardie was one of the last Grimsby trawler skippers to defy Iceland's declaration of exclusive fishing rights over an area two hundred miles from its coast, in what had previously been international waters. Icelandic gunboats towing net cutters would slice through the steel cables British trawlers used to drag their nets behind them, while Royal Navy frigates tried to keep the gunboats away. Hardie was fishing with a group of twenty trawlers one afternoon, dragging his nets at the standard three and a half knots, when a gunboat bore down on them, twice as big as their boat and going at six times the speed. There was no way to manoeuvre, and hauling in the nets took half an hour. All Hardie could do when he realised the gunboat had picked out his vessel was yell at his crew to clear the deck in case the severed cable whiplashed back. The gunboat swept past tight across their stern, the cable went slack, and their net and all the fish it contained sank to the bottom of the Atlantic.

Soon afterwards, in 1976, under pressure from the United States and Britain's military chiefs, who took seriously Iceland's threats to opt out of the North Atlantic surveillance chain monitoring the Soviet nuclear submarine fleet, London effectively surrendered the two-hundred-mile zone to Reykjavik. Cruelly, the man obliged to seal the deal was the Labour MP for Grimsby, the then foreign secretary, Anthony Crosland.

Barred from the rich fisheries off Iceland, Hardie turned to Norway, which, although it was outside the EEC, offered

EEC fishing vessels the chance to fish there under a quota system negotiated through Brussels.* One time he arrived off Norway with quota to spare only to get a message from his company saying that because a French vessel had over-fished, the Norwegians were cutting the quota of another EEC boat – which happened to be his. The only way he could cover his costs was to take his trawler into the perilous waters of the Arctic, above the 72nd parallel.

Hardie didn't resent Iceland and Norway for the way they asserted control over their two-hundred-mile waters. He envied them. He held, with Ukip, that if Britain had stayed outside the EEC, as Iceland and Norway did, Britain could have had its own two-hundred-mile zone, and the three countries could have carved up the North Sea and North Atlantic between them. Instead, Grimsby trawlermen had to share with the Spanish, the French, the Danes and the Dutch and endure a European quota regime supposed to conserve fish stocks that until recently obliged them, when they caught the wrong fish, to dump it.

As I listened to Hardie I thought of something John Fenty, the local businessman who owned Grimsby Town Football Club, had told me a couple of days earlier: how he got his start in 1984 hiring transport out to a local trader who drove around the colliery villages inland, selling fish factory discards to striking miners. I asked Hardie about the miners

---

* Britain voted in a referendum to join the European Economic Community in 1975. The transformation of the EEC into the European Union began with the Treaty of Maastricht in 1992 and was completed by the Treaty of Lisbon in 2009. No referendum was held in Britain on either treaty, although John Major's Conservatives were re-elected after he signed the Maastricht Treaty.

and he knew what I was getting at. 'I feel for the mining industry,' he said. 'I feel for them because it's the same as what happened to the fishing industry.'

On an electoral map illustrating a Matthew Goodwin article, the blighted English fishing constituencies – Grimsby, Hull, Great Yarmouth – were included among Ukip's target seats. But there was something awfully familiar about the deep purple blotches elsewhere on the map: South Wales, Nottinghamshire, South Yorkshire, County Durham. The places where most of Britain's coal miners worked before the strike of 1984–85 (there were 180,000 miners then; now, fewer than two thousand) overlapped strikingly with the traditional Labour constituencies where Ukip support was strongest. Miners and fishermen, two groups of skilled workers winning goods from nature, exploited and well paid at the same time, doing hard jobs that women didn't do, for whom the danger was not only a source of menace but also of pride, a way to test your manhood in front of other men. They might recoil instinctively from Nigel Farage, but they could say that since the coal stopped and the fish stopped, the implied utterance from London government to miners and fishermen has been: 'What, are you still here?'*

It's not that they don't still fish out of Grimsby. One morning I met Andrew Allard, who ran a ten-vessel outfit called Jubilee Fishing from an office in the docks. When he showed me on a map on the wall where his boats were at that moment I got a sense of the big world of the Grimsby fishermen, how

---

* In the Brexit referendum of 2016, the English and Welsh coalfield districts would vote by 62 per cent to 38 per cent to leave the EU, ten points higher than the national result.

unprovincial it had been to roam the far corners of Canute's old North Sea Empire. One boat had just landed cod, haddock and monkfish in Peterhead, another was fishing for plaice off Denmark, another was taking shelter from gales in Orkney. 'He'll stay there till lunchtime, till it's blown through. It was blowing seventy miles an hour, that's a bit naughty.'

Allard had no ideological problem with Ukip, including their policies on immigration – 'I know we're at the end of a railway line, and not many people want to come here, and I'm OK with that' – but that didn't mean he was going to vote for them. Sceptical about Labour's economic management (at this point Labour was still headed by Ed Miliband, portrayed by the Conservative media as dangerously left-wing), Allard was leaning Tory. 'During most government terms you generally get a protest vote and then, when it comes to the big one, people revert,' he said.

He was still waiting for a credible explanation of how pulling out of the EU would bring a restoration of vanished days. 'The Cod War thing was before my time,' he said. 'I joined when it had been and gone, the late Seventies, and gradually saw the harbour year by year emptying of fishing boats . . . If we'd been in charge of our own waters like the Norwegians and Iceland I think we would still see a vibrant catching industry round here. But the reality is we joined Europe . . . You can't just say: "We're quitting, we're going to announce a two-hundred-mile limit." You would have to be clear about the scenario if we came out.'

There was a story of economic ruin in Grimsby. But it wasn't the one Ukip told. The truth is that fishing's decline predated the Cod War and Britain's EEC membership. The sharpest fall in the number of full-time fishermen in England after the Second World War was between 1948 and 1960, when it slumped from 26,000 to fewer than 13,000. After that the fall was steady but slow. Statistics make a poor meal for a hungry family, and are no comfort to the workless, but since 1960, the loss of full-time jobs in the whole English fish-catching business has been, on average, 135 a year.

The myth is that had Britain followed Iceland's example, declared its own two-hundred-mile fishing zone, stayed out of Europe and kept foreigners out of its waters, the harbours of Grimsby and Fleetwood would be as packed with trawlers as in the good old days, whenever those were. The truth is that the Cod War was not about some Little Icelander vision of economic autarky, but Iceland trying desperately to impose control over unrestricted trawling – including by its own boats – that was taking more fish out of the sea than the sea had to give.

Canada also imposed a two-hundred-mile exclusive fishing zone in 1976, gaining control over the rich cod grounds of the Grand Banks for its Newfoundland trawlermen. Canada and Iceland took radically different approaches to steward-ship. The Canadians reckoned that banishing the foreigners meant Canadian fishermen could help themselves to as much cod as they wanted. The result was overfishing on a heroic scale, followed by catastrophe: the Grand Banks cod was almost wiped out. Ottawa imposed a ban on fishing cod in 1992. Meanwhile Iceland, accepting from the start that cod stocks in its waters were perilously depleted, experimented with increasingly sophisticated forms of quota. Over time, fish catches and fish stocks moved closer to equilibrium.

We can't know which version Britain would have gone for if it had stayed out of the EEC and imposed its own two-hundred-mile zone. What we do know is that lots of people would have lost their jobs either way. In Newfoundland and nearby regions, 45,000 jobs were lost almost overnight. In Iceland, the change was gradual but – for a country that only has a hundred thousand men of working age – no less profound. In the 1980s, fishing in Iceland employed 16,000 people; now, it's 8,000. After the Cod War, Iceland actually shed more fishing jobs, proportionately, than Britain.

Britain did get a two-hundred-mile limit, but it was the EEC's, not Britain's, and what followed was the Common Fisheries Policy, which began as a hamfisted mash-up of the Canadian and the Icelandic approaches, and is now, forty years and thousands of redundancies and ship-scrappings later, beginning to get catches and stocks in line.

Too late for most of Grimsby's fishermen. Yet the fish keeps coming, even if British trawlers aren't bringing it. 'There's more fish coming in to the Humber than there ever was,' Martin Boyers, who ran Grimsby fish market, told me. 'We're still getting Icelandic fish but instead of us catching it they catch it themselves.'

The fish market was a generic low-rise industrial building deep inside the docks. It could have been any industrial unit, anywhere: concrete block walls, low-pitched corrugated steel roof, trailers parked in loading bays behind a spiked steel fence. You'd never know from the outside that inside they were auctioning off the fresh spoils of the chase. When I was there, at seven o'clock one March morning, a small area of a vast concrete-floored shed held rows of yellow boxes filled with fish packed on crushed ice: cod longer than my arm, skate like kites made of mangled flesh, the astonished eyes of haddock. Porters, buyers and auctioneers milled around in white coats and hats and yellow wellies, bidding for lots, marking their purchases with strips of paper. In Britain only Peterhead market was bigger. Boyers lifted haddock up by the eyes – a thumb in one eye, an index finger in the other – to show me the subtle difference in silver scales between fish caught in the North and the Irish Seas. The haddock was going for £1.50 a kilo. The week before it had been £3.50. The price went up and down depending on how stormy it was. Boyers had the weather forecasts for Tromsø and Reykjavik a tap and a swipe away on his smartphone. 'It's the only commodity that people go out and hunt,' he said. 'You can't catch it to order and if the weather's bad, there isn't any.'

Most of the fish was brought from Iceland in a container ship, unloaded at Immingham, ten miles to the north, then brought to Grimsby by truck. Much was bought by supermarkets, and much ended up being cleaned and filleted and skinned and chopped up and packaged in Grimsby, in scores of other concrete and corrugated steel hangars spread out around the town's feeder roads. Grimsby – rich in obscure and hard to verify superlatives – claimed more cold storage than any town in Britain, or, depending on who you were talking to, Europe, or the world. One firm alone, Young's, kings of the frozen fish finger, employed 1,700 people; others were smaller, but there were dozens of them, including one perky outfit that dealt in nothing but cod cheeks and cod tongues.

The food processing factories, and the cargo-handling business of Grimsby and Immingham, Britain's biggest port, together with Immingham's sprawl of refineries and power stations, had kept Grimsby going, but hadn't brought visible prosperity, or a sense of communal prosperity, or statistical prosperity. The constituency had the twenty-third-worst unemployment rate in the country. One in ten Grimbarian men was on the dole. One in four young people had no job. In the Marshes in 2011, the last time the clipboard-carriers peered down to that level of detail, unemployment was running at 20 per cent. For those in low-paid work, the introduction of zero-hours contracts and agencies, which prevailed in food plants, were turning pensions, paid time off and job protection into luxuries.

The Ukip narrative of fishing's collapse was not only inaccurate, however. It also projected pessimism too widely over Grimsby's economic future. I found pockets of optimism. An unexpected new source of work had appeared, skilled work that matched brawn and endurance with extreme engineering finesse. Essentially Grimsby hoped to become to wind power what Aberdeen became to the North Sea oil industry. There was an offshore wind rush on, primed by green taxes collected by private power firms through electricity bills. Like the movements of catchable fish, wind power was unpredictable; unlike fish, it was inexhaustible. While there was only one common two-hundred-mile Eurolimit for fish, national two-hundred-mile zones remained in place for wind farms, and Britain's zone is vast. Wind power has the potential to give Grimsby back a sense that seemed lost for ever, a sense of the sea as its domain. Four of the big wind power firms – Siemens, Centrica, Dong Energy and E.On – had set up bases in the docks, with maintenance boats and survey vessels coming and going. They were renting houses and block-booking B&Bs for their staff; I saw their corporate logos on synthetic fleeces at the bars in the resort of Cleethorpes, to which Grimsby is conjoined. Two wind farms, Lincs and Lynn & Inner Dowsing, were already fully operational off Skegness, south of Grimsby. Two more, Westermost Rough and Humber Gateway, were almost finished to the north. Construction of another three, Triton Knoll, Dudgeon and Race Bank, was about to start.

These were only the prelude to far more ambitious plans, the so-called Round 3 wind farms like Dogger Bank Creyke Beck, a staggeringly grandiose project to plant turbines in the middle of the North Sea over an area almost three times the size of the Isle of Wight, 130 miles north-east of the mouth of the Humber, producing about as much electricity as a mid-sized nuclear reactor. In cost and scale, the North Sea Round 3 wind farms are a £10 billion-plus enterprise, a kind of moon shot against climate change. 'We've seen many an ex-fisherman, deck hands or skippers, converted and gone over to the new industry,' Boyers told me.

It remains to be seen what wind power will do for the fabric of Grimsby, what kind of restoration there might be for the highly gendered culture of the fishing fleet, with its men hunting at sea and its women on shore, the culture of great skill and heroic effort and little classroom learning. There was no place for a woman on a trawler. And ever since the Middle Ages, when Grimsby first began sending members to Parliament, it had sent men. After the election, it was as close to a racing certainty as you could get that Grimsby's MP would be a woman.

To talk about politics and abdication in Grimsby was, for most people, to assume you were talking about Austin Mitchell, the then eighty-year-old Labour MP who was to step down in May after almost four decades. Mitchell won the seat in a by-election in 1977 after Anthony Crosland died suddenly of a brain haemorrhage. Muriel Barker, a veteran local Labour leader who campaigned for both men, told me the intellectual middle-class southerner Crosland had adopted Grimsby as his own, but had over-idealised the town's machismo. 'He liked the working class,' she said. 'I think he was just in love with the concept. I think if he'd seen the women being beaten up when the lads came home from the sea he'd have had a different viewpoint.'

Mitchell, previously an academic and TV interviewer, became the most prominent voice of fishermen in Westminster, and helped Billy Hardie's mother, Dolly, in her successful campaign to get compensation for fishermen who lost their livelihoods after the Cod War. He was first elected as European restrictions on Britain's fish catching began to bite, and talked up withdrawal from Europe long before Ukip appeared on the scene. In the early 1980s, in Michael Foot's Labour Party, quitting the EEC was policy. When Neil Kinnock took over, Labour embraced Europe, but Mitchell didn't. His banishment to the back benches as the epitome of old Labour – a socialist, an internationalist and localist rather than globalist, a believer in higher taxation and higher public spending, a champion of the working class, a sceptic on Europe, a conservative on gender – came about after he infuriated Kinnock with what would now be seen as a rather New Labour move. He took the Murdoch shilling, signing up as the leftie to Norman Tebbit's Tory on Sky's 1990s *Crossfire* knockoff, *Target*.

Mitchell's successor was almost certain be one of two women, Labour's Melanie Onn, or Ukip's Victoria Ayling. The polls had Onn edging it, but it looked close. Though Mitchell was stepping back from politics his legacy haunted both parties. Ayling was chosen by Ukip as the candidate who almost beat Mitchell in 2010, when she ran against him as a Conservative. Yet the choice had alienated the left-wing Ukip members in Grimsby who were its most effective campaigners, people who drew on Mitchell's own paradigm of socialist anti-EU rhetoric. Onn, meanwhile, was selected from an all-woman shortlist of Labour candidates. The imposition on the local party of a woman-only list had soured the campaign; there was resentment that long-serving local Labour men were kept out of the running.

Rather than stand aloof, Mitchell weighed in. In a piece for the *Daily Mail* the previous August, a month after Onn was selected, he talked of Ed Miliband's aide Anna Yearley orchestrating 'the feminisation of Labour'. He went on: 'Yearley believes that the best man for any job, except perhaps the Pope, is a woman . . . Most selections are now on the all-women basis, even where hairy-arsed local politics, a major Ukip threat or a substantial Muslim population might suggest that it's better to choose a man.' Women, he added, were interested in 'small problems rather than big ideas and issues'.

When I met him, sitting at his cluttered desk in a big homely Victorian terraced house in Grimsby, he was emollient, and praised Onn as 'a very good candidate'. But he wouldn't recant. 'I'm assumed to be anti-woman because I opposed an all-woman shortlist,' he grumbled. 'The point was we needed a large entry because the party needed a good choice. Cleethorpes had fourteen [prospective candidates] with an open selection. We had four.'

Onn avoided criticising Mitchell directly after his *Mail* outburst, which reads as a wounded personal cry against ageism as much as a diatribe against gendermandering.* I learned from Labour sources that, following this and other outbursts, senior party figures staged a forceful intervention to get him to sweeten his rhetoric, asking him whether he really wanted Victoria Ayling to be the first Ukip MP for Grimsby.

'We had our minds on other [candidates],' Muriel Barker said. 'But once it's done, it's done, you will line up behind someone who's turned out to be extremely good. [Onn] pinched all the moral ground from Austin because of his stupid remarks but she did it like a little statesman. She wouldn't attack Austin; she said it was uncomfortable, but let's keep our eyes on the prize, let's win. You could have easily descended to silly politics, because Austin needed his legs smacking.'

The after-echoes of the all-woman shortlist row lingered on, in the party and on the doorstep. It was a sign of Labour's deeper problem in Grimsby. As odd as Mitchell's assertion was that women politicians aren't interested in 'big issues' (Thatcher? Merkel?), it was less significant than the joking style of the article and the fact he felt it was a good idea to write it. It was written in the style and the spirit of the move-ment against political correctness, in resistance to a perceived overarching Authority that is out to stop people telling the truth about, or telling jokes about, groups they don't like. Mitchell has always been an antic figure. He once changed his name by deed poll to Austin Haddock to promote the seafood

----

*   The population of the UK is about 49 per cent men and 51 per cent women. The ratio in the House of Commons after the 2017 election was 68:32. Party leaders could have shifted the balance in the unelected House of Lords, but have chosen not to: since 1997, 74 per cent of new peers created to sit in the Lords have been men.

industry. He hasn't been ambitious or radical or vain enough to be accused of the sin of which the likes of Beppe Grillo, Vladimir Zhirinovsky and Nigel Farage are guilty – the uneasy merger of the comedian's claim to offend harmlessly with the politician's claim to need power to save the country. But the movement against political correctness is an essential marker of the Ukip way of looking at things. It is also extremely popular. And if political correctness was seen as strongly bound to Labour, the Lib Dems, David Cameron, the EU, the BBC, the *Guardian* and, in Grimsby, Melanie Onn, the movement against it was strongly connected to Ukip, Jeremy Clarkson, the *Daily Mail* and, in Grimsby, Austin Mitchell.

Before he stood aside, there was speculation Mitchell would be the first Labour MP to defect to Ukip. It didn't happen. He told me that Ukip was 'a fart on the political stage' and that he was 'Labour in the essence of my being'. Still, the tone of his discourse was 'I'm Labour, but . . .'

'I think we're wrong in not offering a referendum on European membership,' he said. 'Some of Ukip's policies are OK. Some are crazy. I think they're right to say we have to be able to manage immigration, we can't just open the floodgates. I think they're right to say we need a degree of distance and more ability to control our destiny. I think they're right to say the Common Fisheries Policy was a disaster that robbed us of food and jobs. They're right to say the Common Agricultural Policy makes food too dear . . .'

I was beginning to think he'd forgotten the crazy policies.

'. . . they're wrong to say it all depends on Europe.'

In the early 1950s, Mitchell pointed out, more than 90 per cent of the British electorate voted Labour or Conservative.

Now it was two-thirds. 'It means a third of the electorate is pissed off with the two main parties and pissed off with politics and pissed off with politicians. Their choice is not voting, or Ukip voting. A lot of them will come from Labour, and their main interests lie in Labour . . . Their world has been destroyed, largely by Thatcherism, but also by us. We went along with this free market economics, we believed we had a new paradigm and would have exponential growth, and we were wrong.'

On the morning I left my B&B to meet the Labour campaign, the three top items on the BBC news were about showbusiness: the crash of a helicopter full of reality TV stars, the *Blurred Lines* plagiarism case and, the lead story, the TV presenter Jeremy Clarkson punching his producer in the face because he couldn't get him a steak dinner after hours.

'They're making a hell of a fuss about Clarkson,' I said to the driver as I got into the cab. 'Why do people care so much?'

'Tells the truth, don't he.'

Labour's Grimsby campaign HQ was a two-storey building on a through road running parallel to the docks. The party bought it off the GMB union. It cost £100 a week to run. It wasn't much to look at from the outside, and the shop window – with its larger than life photo of Onn and the red and yellow posters urging passers-by to Make It Melanie – was covered in a layer of grime. Inside it was spacious, high-ceilinged, full of natural light, swallowing up people and furniture and boxes of leaflets. In the main room on the ground floor rows of chairs and a praesidium table were set out as if for a public meeting. The walls were hung with pictures of past battles and heroes. There was a copy of a campaign poster for Tom Proctor, who ran in Grimsby in 1906 as a candidate for Labour's precursor, the Labour Representation Committee. He came third. His campaign pledges were 'No tax on food, votes for the workless, pension for the aged, fair play all round.'

Steve Elliott was Mitchell's agent in the 2010 campaign. In 2015 he was doing the job for Onn. He was born to socialist parents in a long-demolished slum in the Marshes in the 1950s. He had a white beard and a wan resilience. 'I'm the guy who goes to prison if we spend too much money,' he said. Too much, in Elliott's interpretation of the law, being anything over £32,000 per party, per constituency. In Labour's case much of that came in kind from the unions, in the form of staff hours and mailings.

'We've had an MP for the last thirty-odd years who's been consistently anti-Europe,' Elliott said. 'His views tend to be from the left of centre opposition to the European Union. He believes if we got out of the EU we could renationalise the railways, we could do things our way, we could have a socialist Britain . . . When Ukip came along they latched on to him. They said if you want to support good old Austin, vote Ukip.'

Onn arrived, a pink-cheeked thirty-five-year-old who worked as an organiser for the union Unison. She was late; her car had been stolen. The thief had walked into her house, taken the keys and driven off without her noticing. It hadn't put her off her stride. She was thoughtful and intelligent, careful and distant, and wasn't trying hard to be liked. It hadn't been easy to get her to agree to meet me. Her rise has been against the odds. She was born on a Grimsby council estate, moved away with her mother to London as a small child, and was then separated from her mother and raised back in Grimsby by her great-aunt. She sat her A-levels while living in a hostel for homeless teenagers after her relationship with her great-aunt broke down. She never knew her father; she found out recently that he'd died when she came across his obituary in the Grimsby *Telegraph*. The benefits of the caring state are not abstract concepts to her.

'If there hadn't been education for as long as I wanted, if there hadn't been good-quality social housing, if I hadn't had the opportunity to go to university, if there hadn't been the medical support, the social support – I was on benefits twice – if that hadn't been there, there's no way I would have been where I am now,' she said. 'Now . . . all the things that provide a level playing field for working-class kids just seem to be being taken away.'

Onn didn't deny Labour's complicity in what had happened. It made her campaign a difficult proposition, hard to characterise as anything but 'Please trust us one more time.'

'Labour is now saying there's too much [pressure] on the NHS and the accusation is quickly thrown back at us "it started on your watch" and it's not easy to overcome because it's accurate . . . I think there's a whole new breed of people seeking election. We have seen mistakes that have happened in the last Labour government. We want to get back to the Labour Party that said it wanted to be a party that represented working people and people less able to support themselves.'

It wasn't hard to see why Onn was wary of me. Not only did she have to fight off Ukip at the polls; she had to deal with the festering aftermath of the woman-only selection row and, inside her own party, heads being turned by the allure of a local Ukip that was flying with a strong right wing and a pumped-up, mutant left one. In 2013 a Labour councillor in Grimsby, Jane Bramley, defected to Ukip, saying it was a 'fairer' party. At the 2014 council elections, Ukip gave Labour a drubbing, reducing it to a minority administration. Yet when Labour needed backing to pass its budget this year, Ukip members lined up alongside them against the Conservatives and Lib Dems.

Ray Sutton, chairman of the Great Grimsby Constituency Labour Party, told me: 'I know Ukip have got people who are socialist through and through.' Sutton didn't pretend he wasn't still bothered by the all-woman shortlist, unless distinguishing between his official and personal selves counts as pretence. 'As constituency party chair I accept the party has this policy, and we've operated within that . . . We've ended up with a very good candidate,' he said. 'Personally . . . it's amazing that the 2010 Equality Act has a special law for parliamentary elections. The politicians are doing what nobody else can do . . . it's something I can't come to terms with. I don't raise it with anybody, but people raise it with me.'

I met Sutton in the same room in Labour campaign HQ where I met Onn and Elliott. They'd left us, but though Sutton was forthcoming, and could see I was writing down what he said, he seemed nervous. At one point he looked round to see Phil Pocknee, one of the young Labour volunteers, sitting behind him, and asked if he was there to listen in. Pocknee, a student, seemed embarrassed to think Sutton should imagine such a thing, and left. Whether Sutton was being unduly anxious, or Pocknee really was monitoring dissent, it suggested Labour's small ship – the party in Grimsby had two hundred members – didn't have a happy crew.

Ukip seemed well placed to take advantage. Yet as much as Victoria Ayling talked up Labour's all-woman shortlist kerfuffle – 'As a female can I just say among my friends and female politicians generally we don't need this patronising attitude' – her position within her own local party looked less secure than Onn's within hers. Grimsby Ukip was all about a localist approach to national problems, but Ayling was the only one of the candidates who wasn't born and raised in the town. Even the Conservative candidate, Marc Jones, was born to a staunch Labour family in East Marsh. Ayling was from South London, and only moved to rural Lincolnshire, south of Grimsby, in the 2000s (she did have a spell in Hull early in her career, marketing cod liver oil).

She also faced accusations of racism. The *Mail on Sunday* got hold of a promotional video from 2008, when she was still a Conservative, in which she talks about immigrants. Between takes she says as an aside: 'I just want to send the lot back, but I can't say that.' Ayling claims she was talking about illegal immigrants. This is not obvious from the video. The same newspaper claimed Ayling had been a member of the National Front in the late 1970s. Ayling denies she was a member, but admits having gone to meetings, saying she was carrying out research for a thesis.

Ayling came to Grimsby from local politics in the Lincolnshire countryside, where her opposition to the twenty small wind turbines generating electricity in the fields at Conisholme was an uncontroversial, even popular stance: 'Click here to email us if you can hear the turbine blades swishing at night,' urged the website of the Louth *Leader* in

2008. She then transferred her hostility from rural windmills to the gargantuan industrial project to reap the winds far offshore in the North Sea, where a single turbine will generate almost as much power as the whole Conisholme wind farm. During Round 3 more than two thousand of them are supposed to be planted in the seabed, each of their three blades longer than the wingspan of a jumbo jet. Ayling insisted on the folly of wind power – its unreliability, its cost, its insignificant contribution to the local economy – even as Grimsby was fighting with other ports to be its champion. Listening to Ayling diss wind power was like hearing a resident who lived under the flight path of a local flying club trying to persuade Heathrow's 76,000 workers to vote for her so she could shut the airport down.

Nationally, the party was on her side. One of Ukip's unambiguous policies was to abolish 'green taxes', a small part of which, typically £2.50 a month on a household electricity bill (the amount will rise), goes to subsidise wind farms, solar energy, biomass generation and, in future, nuclear power. The cost of offshore wind farming, even without factoring in reduced pollution and carbon emissions, is on a steady downward curve, but a Ukip government would have killed the industry instantly, as well as making new nuclear power stations impossible.

When I arrived in Grimsby it seemed likely the local election campaign had already seen its two memorable moments. One was Mitchell telling the *Independent on Sunday* that the town's seat was so safely Labour the party would win even if it selected as its candidate a 'raving alcoholic sex paedophile'. The other was a clash at a local hustings over wind power between Ayling and the Green candidate, Vicky Dunn. Greens tend to be stereotyped as head-in-the-clouds tree-hugging Luddites who would rather see a city devastated by unemployment than harm the habitat of a single puffin, but Dunn is a no-nonsense northern gearhead Green who told me, when I asked about the future of the steelworks in nearby Scunthorpe, that the steel for wind turbine shafts would have to be made somewhere. When Dunn and Ayling went head to head it was Ayling who came across as the oddball.

DUNN (*to Ayling*): People in Grimsby remember that the fishing industry was stabbed in the back by politicians. I'm very concerned that you're a politician that is lining up to walk down the docks and stab our new industry in the back.

AYLING: Certainly not. Because these renewables will not last for ever. The subsidies will dry up and when the subsidies . . .

DUNN: That's kind of the point. (*Audience laughter*)

Although Ayling didn't use the exact words, the Twitterverse has made sure she will always be remembered as saying: 'What happens when the renewables run out?'

The Ayling–Dunn exchange had the lexicon of a disagreement about economics and science, but the expressive mood of clashing belief systems and a shared disgust with a political status quo that blocks the triumph of passion over cost–benefit analysis. Dunn's belief in the all-consuming primacy of climate change and Ayling's belief that climate change is a lie divided them. But they were united by a desire for the kind of disruptive change that makes the Wagyu sirloin turn to ash in the mouths of fund managers.

Trying to describe the mood of the electorate, and why they were drawn to Ukip, Dunn told me: 'It's about emotions, it's about anger . . . [The truth] is not something you can easily persuade people of with statistics. That's not what they listen to any more. They've got a feeling something's not right. Which, interestingly enough, is something which drives the Green vote as well.'

I met Ayling in Freeman Street Market, a refurbished space which stood out in the retail desolation of East Marsh for having had money spent on it. Ukip Grimsby had its base there in a temporary wood and glass pavilion of the kind you see at trade fairs. It was clean and bright and neatly spread with purple and yellow leaflets. Too neatly: the place lacked the healthy turmoil of an insurgent campaign in high gear. Ayling had a bright-eyed zeal. She was friendly and good-humoured. She seemed to draw comfort from having come to rest in a place of absolute political certainty and hewed to her policy lines as if by repeating them often enough she would make the scales of doubt fall from my sceptical metropolitan eyes and compel me to follow her to a better realm where good English common sense prevailed.

She turned against Cameron in 2009 when he cancelled his pledge, if elected, to hold a referendum on the Lisbon Treaty. But four years passed before she left the Conservatives. 'I felt he was just weak and doing anything to please his European masters. In March 2013, at the Spring Forum, he was spreading his lies and spin about how he controlled immigration. I went up to him, stopped him in his tracks and told him he was a traitor; he was disingenuous, and not fit to run the country, and I was going to Ukip. He was stunned into silence. He stood frozen to the spot as his security people pulled me away from him. They thought I was going to assassinate him . . . I've been a Tory since I was fourteen and it was a big, big step to take . . . I can't live a lie any more, I can't follow the blue any more with this man at the helm.'

Ayling was a human definition of chutzpah. It took chutzpah to sit in the middle of East Marsh, one of the poorest wards in Europe, and say: 'I'm pro-austerity, as long as it's targeted properly.' It took chutzpah to say about global warming, in a place almost devastated by a storm surge little more than a year earlier: 'I think it's a lot of nonsense. I think it's a con. Climate change is an excuse to tax people.' It took chutzpah to tell me the lie that leaving Europe would save Britain £55 million a day when refurbishment of the market hosting her was 50 per cent funded by repatriated EU money.

Most of all it took chutzpah to denigrate the industry that seemed to offer the best hope of revival to the town where she was running for office. Ayling didn't back down a milli-watt on her stance at the hustings. Wind power had generated 9.3 per cent of Britain's electricity the year before,* yet Ayling called it 'unreliable', because the wind didn't blow all the time – in the way, presumably, that fishing was unreliable, because sometimes the trawlermen went out and didn't catch anything. 'I do not want to have subsidies paid into something unreliable,' she said. 'I would like to have wind subsidies cut. I do believe it's a passing fad. I'm concerned

---

* By 2019, this had risen to 20 per cent.

we, as a town, are going to be too dependent on something that may go tomorrow, and what then?'

The fourth woman running for the Great Grimsby seat was Val O'Flynn, the ex-Militant Tendency candidate for the radical left-wing Trade Unionist and Socialist Coalition. I met her one Friday lunchtime in a sprawling hotel bar near Grimsby Town station where mothers with pushchairs and plates of food shared space with tottering, booze-darkened drinkers. We talked for a while about TUSC, its desire for a socialist transformation of society and its policy of quitting the EU – 'nothing more than a pro-business, neoliberal organisation'. I could see, when she talked about immigration, what a gaping space there was on the radical left for Ukip to enter. The open door immigration policy, she said, 'suited the capitalist because it increases the labour force, it has a downward effect on wages, and immigrants are much easier to exploit. Immigrants come over here partly because of the faults of capitalism in their own countries. What is a minimum wage here is a good wage compared to what it would be at home. That brings the wages down for the rest of us.'

I asked her about Ukip. 'Ukip is very divided here,' she said. 'I know branch members of Ukip who are locals who can't stand Victoria Ayling. She was parachuted in.' I suddenly remembered a bit of gossip somebody had told me about O'Flynn. Wasn't she . . .

She smiled. 'I'm engaged to a Ukip man,' she said. To Chris Osborne, in fact, the campaign manager for Steve Harness, Ukip candidate for Cleethorpes. They met over a shared cause. 'I've been banned from Morrison's for doing a protest about them selling Israeli goods and Chris has been sort of fighting this pro-Palestine corner for years so that's how we got talking.' He would have been very much at home in the old Labour Party, she said.

I asked if I could meet him, and we got in a taxi. Osborne, a gentle, silver-haired man in a baggy black T-shirt, ran a tattoo parlour he co-owned in Cleethorpes. He sat down sheepishly next to his pink and blue-haired fiancée on a bench in the window and explained how he'd converted to Ukip after an encounter with Paul Nuttall, then the party's deputy leader, at a public meeting last year. Nuttall assured him that if he joined, he wouldn't have to follow a central party line – he could campaign on local issues in his own way. 'I had no interest in Ukip,' he said. 'All I'd seen was what everybody else had seen, Nigel Farage, his pint and his fag. But I was told you best represent Ukip by representing your community, and I like that. Ukip up here are largely ex-Labour. Up here is a far more grass-roots, hard working-class background than it is down south.

'I was a Labour member for many, many years. I was at Orgreave and I was a steel worker at Scunthorpe during the strike of 1980, on the picket lines. But I've become increasingly disillusioned. When New Labour came along it just became "We are the Conservatives." I drifted away from the party.'

We chatted for a while. You often hear people from Scotland talking about how exciting it was in the run-up to the 2014 Independence referendum to have the country turned into one big political discussion group, well-informed, passionate and reasonable, and it was a bit like that, except that when I'd imagined something similar happening in England, I hadn't put a Ukip activist in there. O'Flynn and Osborne sparred in an edgy way, and as they performed people who came in for their tattoos sat and listened quietly.

'I'm fiercely, fiercely anti-racist,' Osborne said. 'We are aware that we have had people back in the south, very English, who have expressed ridiculous sentiments and have to be weeded out. Ukip is still in a state of evolution. Twenty-two Labour MPs voted against same-sex marriage but nobody says they're homophobic.'

'Clause 4 was removed,' said O'Flynn. 'They embraced neoliberalism. We were betrayed, totally betrayed by the Labour Party.'

OSBORNE: People are working on these ridiculous zero-hours contracts, working for next to nothing, it's an abomination. The main reason I'm not in TUSC . . . we have a lot of common ground, fighting for people at the bottom. But the organised socialism side of it leaves me a little cold.

O'FLYNN: He's not a revolutionary.

OSBORNE: We've made great strides in the north of England. The Labour heartlands are stopping being Labour heartlands.

O'FLYNN: Ukip is making it OK for people to come out and be racist.

OSBORNE: We cut down immigration, we make the unskilled worker more valuable.

O'FLYNN: But then you're putting the focus on the immigrants rather than the employers.

OSBORNE: The Labour Party, for me, was a sacrosanct thing. It stood between the working man and the bottomless pit of poverty. It became about being elected.

O'FLYNN: All Ukip seems to be interested in is getting rid of anything that impacts business. I think you're delusional.

A few days after I left Grimsby, there was another leak. The *Sunday Mirror* got hold of a recording of a showdown between the neo-socialist local Ukippers and a party official over the lack of support for Ayling. On the tape, Osborne is heard to describe Ayling as 'possibly the worst candidate we could have'. He says: 'I cannot endorse or support a candidate who I genuinely believe – whether anybody else does or not – who I genuinely believe is racist.'

In the recent past the word 'disruptive' was a euphemism for 'troublesome', but in the language of those who write about society, technology and finance, it's come to have the positive meaning of 'transformational', as in 'Uber has had a disruptive effect on the old taxi cartels.' Martin Boyers called Ukip's rise the 'Lidl effect', after the discount chain's disruption of the complacent empires of Tesco and Sainsbury's. Ukip, the Greens and TUSC offered the disruption so many voters seem to want, but wouldn't get the national votes to deliver it. The Conservatives, Labour and the Lib Dems would get the votes, but didn't offer disruption; they pledged to avoid it, bidding to manage the country in the best way, for the lowest price, with a few customer service tweaks, like train company operators bidding for a franchise – free wifi, complimentary drinks in first class. For all the talk of the 99 per cent, as long as at least 51 per cent of voters were content with the no-disruption parties, they won. The only party to combine vote-winning potential with the promise of disruptive change was a party that wasn't running in Grimsby, the Scottish National Party.

This left Grimsby with a problem, because the established parties had, in the name of no-disruption good stewardship, engineered a disruptive transformation in the way political power was exercised in small English towns. It was a change so massive and so gradual that neither the politicians involved, nor the citizens of those towns, nor even those exercising the power, were ready to acknowledge that it had happened. The great abdication in Grimsby was of power itself, local power, an essential trinity of access to resources, inspired, ruthless marshalling of effort, and care for what local people think. There was an abundance of autonomy in Grimsby, some of it remarkable and interesting. But local autonomy isn't the same as local power.

In Grimsby, you could see the effects of two old disruptions that had unintended consequences. Thatcher hoped that privatisation would create globe-straddling British companies owned by small British shareholders, but instead most of the privatised firms and their small shareholders had been bought out by foreign governments and overseas pension funds. The ports of Grimsby and Immingham, for instance, used to be owned by the British public. Then they were privatised, with shares sold to anyone with the means and will to buy them. Then the shareholders were bought out by their present owners, Associated British Ports, a conglomerate which, in turn, is almost entirely owned by Canadian pension funds and the governments of Singapore and Kuwait.

The second disruption was the set of changes brought about by Blair's Third Way. They were supposed to force new ideas into health, education and social housing. Instead, they were seized on by the Conservatives in 2010 as the vehicle to separate the welfare state from the state that created it. The NHS and the education system were split into autonomous, commercialised units with incentives to merge and form chains; housing associations were simply starved of cash to build homes. In Grimsby, in Anthony Crosland's old constituency, the comprehensive school is no more. Each of the area's ten state secondary schools has become an academy; six are part of national chains, administered from offices in Birmingham, London, Leeds and Grantham. It's not that they aren't doing good work – they may be – but they are part of a landscape of local political power entirely different from the one the election candidates and the media speak to, the one citizens still believe exists. For most people in Grimsby, when something big goes wrong, blame goes to 'the government', or 'the council' – in Grimsby's case, the authority of North-East Lincolnshire, which covers Grimsby, Cleethorpes and Immingham.

'The local authority is in a very invidious position because it has no control over schools, but is held accountable,' said David Hampson, who runs a local academy chain, the Tollbar Family of Academies, with two secondary schools and a sixth-form college. Tony Bramley, the head of Shoreline, told me: 'The public will just see the NHS and the council and the police. Many people still think we are the council.'

Even though Labour masterminded the mass transfer of council houses to Shoreline, and introduced academies and NHS trusts, it tried to make sure something was holding it all together. 'We all had to have a plan,' Bramley said. 'It was, if you like, structured and enforced by government officials. There were key performance indicators. Everybody got judged and ranked and we all resisted and kicked against it because we thought it was a top-down, centralised method. All that went in 2010 when the new government came in. The immediate reaction was a weight lifted off everybody's shoulders. Then ... combine a lack of direction with the fragmentation that has happened. When you want to talk to anyone it's very difficult. Some do, some don't. Without local authority goals it becomes much more difficult.'

Along with the fragmentation of power into sectoral fiefdoms is the hulking presence of Associated British Ports, known to all locally as ABP. From the window of Bramley's office we could see thousands of identical white Toyotas, made in Derby, and the car carrier they were about to be loaded onto for shipment to the Continent. With Immingham and Killingholme, Grimsby was Britain's biggest port for importing and exporting cars.

'The issue is ABP's control of the waterfront,' Bramley said. 'It locks the community away from the sea in large parts of the borough. Obviously it's a private company with its own business model but Grimsby, Cleethorpes and Immingham have not been able to take advantage of their natural asset to the extent many other places have because of this unfair private sector control of that very key aspect. It's a very big economic generator but it has a real impact on the ability of the community to help the town.'

The free burghers of Grimsby got their charter from King John in 1201, but the original harbour silted up in medieval times, the town went into decline, and by the nineteenth century it was a notorious rotten borough with a few hundred hereditary freemen choosing two MPs. The great fishing boom, and the current shape of the town, dates back only as far as the middle of the nineteenth century, when the Manchester, Sheffield and Lincolnshire Railway Company laid a line through the Marshes and built the grand network of docks linking the mouth of the Humber with the River Freshney.

'Before the port was built, it was a hamlet,' said John Fitzgerald, who ran ABP's Humber ports. 'Then two and a half thousand Irish navvies came with spades.' The fishermen who flocked to populate East and West Marsh in the 1850s and 1860s were immigrants from other parts of Britain, most of them – coincidentally or not – from fishing ports in Essex and Kent where Ukip support runs high today.

On the eve of the 2015 election, between the thriving waterfront – where the cars were transhipped, the fish were auctioned and the wind farmers were gearing up to sow the sea with turbines – and the just about bustling, pre-industrial Top Town district, where the main shopping centre was, lay the decaying streets of East Marsh, leading straight to the acres of desolation of the ice factory and its environs. Near the ice factory were the streets where the turnstones foraged, handsome, damp, cracked frontages of dark brick, with boarded-up windows and weeds growing out of the gutters. The odd puff from a smokehouse chimney or pile of polystyrene fishboxes showed where commerce persisted, but the general atmosphere was of a place waiting to host the final shootout scene of a 1970s cop drama. It was a strange thrill to look up at the street signs, see they had the ABP logo on them, and realise I was on ABP territory. They looked like public British streets, but were, in fact, private. Was I even in Britain? Or was I in a globalist anomaly, one-third Singapore, 58 per cent Canada? John Fitzgerald told me that the doubly privatised ABP was good for Grimsby, and good for Britain. Yet the government of Singapore still owned the port of Singapore, and the Canadian state still owned the ports of Canada. ABP, which had a virtual monopoly on the Humber, Britain's busiest trading estuary, recently went all the way to Parliament to try to block an entrepreneur's plan to build a new port near Immingham to stage the turbines and masts for the Round 3 wind farms. Fitzgerald said he had £500 million to spend on new projects in the Humber, but his position as steward of one of Canada and Singapore's far-flung estates didn't permit him to set money aside to mend the roof of the ice factory. 'We're happy to talk to anybody who has a plan for it,' he said. 'Ultimately, the renovation of a building like that is not a business we are in.'

I found a popular idea in Grimsby, as in so many other small towns across the country, that what was needed, all that was really needed, was jobs. Something would open, bringing jobs. Something would close, and jobs would be lost. Jobs joy, jobs gloom. Nothing must be done to destroy jobs. Everything must be done to attract jobs. 'Jobs' having nothing to do with the job you actually had, or the job you wanted but couldn't get. 'Jobs' was the magical key to communal contentment, to Freeman Street lighting up with chain stores, to nice clothes and holidays and happy children. For sure, the town was desperately in need of work. But there was a problem with the jobs obsession, and not just because so many of the jobs were low-paid, low-skilled, insecure ones. (Grimsby held first place in the country for 'semi-routine' occupations, 'typified', the statisticians said, 'by a short term and the direct exchange of money for effort'.)

There were plenty of jobs during the hundred-year fishing boom; that's what the people of Grimsby believe, anyway. Certainly fortunes were made by successful trawler owners. And yet it was striking how little mark all those jobs and all that capital left on the landscape in terms of great buildings or the endowment of institutes or galleries. Those who grew rich bought farmland, moved away, sent their children to private schools, got the smell of fish out of their clothes. In *A New Kind of Bleak*, Owen Hatherley describes how during its fishing boom years Aberdeen almost bankrupted itself with grand architecture and elaborate cultural legacies, yet 'in the thirty-five years since Aberdeen became the oil capital of Europe, the city has not seen a single worthwhile building in the city centre.' Grimsby was left with much less than Aberdeen from its fishing days, and risks having the wind power boom rush through without bringing anything to the city more rich and lasting than jobs.

There were countless signs in Grimsby that as a town it was somehow incomplete, all skewed one way. In the country as a whole, more than a quarter of the population had higher than school level qualifications. In Grimsby, it was about 15 per cent. Nearly a third of people in Grimsby had no passport, one of the highest proportions in the country. Most of the town's huge collection of maritime art was in storage because the town's only public gallery, in the Fishing Heritage Centre, was tiny. 'We don't get anything new,' Val O'Flynn said. 'New ideas don't come here, or if they do, they're old by the time Grimsby gets them.' David Hampson, of the Tollbar Academies, said his biggest problem with his pupils was lack of aspiration. I asked him about something Muriel Barker had said, that despite all her efforts, Grimsby was still seen as a cultural desert. Hampson seemed surprised anyone would think of looking for culture in Grimsby. 'If I want culture,' he said, 'I go and spend two or three days in another city.'

Tony Bramley of Shoreline said he had always struggled to recruit senior professionals, and the problem wasn't money. He described a meeting where he and a group of private housing developers were talking about the future. 'When it came to the key things that would make this a better place to live, the answer was culture. The answer was not the economy, not a different mix of homes. The answer was: what do people do in the evenings? . . . My big fear, which I keep voicing everywhere I go, is if there is to be a surge of economic activity, primarily on the back of the renewable energy, we will see job growth but not housing growth. They will come here to work but will go back and spend money in other settlements.'

An effort by a local trust to save the ice factory by buying it from ABP and turning it into an art gallery and cinema foundered when the Heritage Lottery Fund turned them down. Meanwhile, on Freeman Street, the hereditary Freemen – they still exist, eight centuries after they got their charter from King John, and still own the freehold of most of the shops on the street that bears their name – had renovated the market, with the EU's help. The council installed new lampposts. Everyone understood they were just pecking away at the rot and that only a determined, well-funded and imaginative vision to transform the entire area and bring the docks and the town together would succeed. But with the local arm of the state, the council, weakened by Third Way disaggregation, ABP essentially a buy-to-let proposition run by absentee landlords in Toronto and Singapore, and with no sign of the kind of buccaneering local capitalists who built the docks in the first place, this looked unlikely.

Rising high above the docks was the one great monument in Grimsby to the old power of local capital, the Grimsby Dock Tower. It was built in 1852 for strictly utilitarian purposes, as the container for a hydraulic system that opened dock gates and operated cranes. The ingenuity of its design was necessary to its function. The beauty of its appearance was not. It was built as a copy of the Torre del Mangia in Siena, but had a ruddy Hanseatic simplicity quite in keeping with the north. It was a boastful flourish added by business-men who were around on the local scene, who cared what local people thought of them, who wanted to impress and awe. The tower remained. No such route to public magnifi-cence existed in the second decade of the twenty-first century. ABP had no reason to perform that kind of boast because Canadian pensioners had no reason to boast to the people of Grimsby. Toronto and Singapore wanted neither to help East Marsh, nor to have the mighty of Grimsby look on their works and despair. They just wanted their five per cent return on equity, as smoothly as possible, thank you.

Would the Round 3 wind farms be different? Ayling made much of fears that the cream of the work would go to outside specialists, particularly foreigners. It's true Round 3 would be built by mainly northern European energy companies who've done a deal with the government similar to the one Électricité de France has made to build nuclear reactors. Their focus is not on cutting a swagger on the Humber and leaving a legacy but on rate of return on investment, global markets and the advancement of continental European technology – there's little British technology in the field. It's also true that subsidies, guaranteeing Round 3 farms three times the regular wholesale price of electricity for fifteen years, were high, and vulnerable to political attack. What wind power offered Grimsby was the prospect of restoring a source of grandeur the town had lost – a harbour filled with working boats. The harder thing was to land something less transient than jobs, that left Grimsby more than memories of a life at sea.

The nearest to any kind of visionary capitalist I found embedded in Grimsby was John Fenty, owner of Grimsby Town Football Club. He also sat as a Conservative on the council. Having made his money in the fish processing business Fenty was trying to get the council to permit a big new housing development on the southern outskirts of town. In return for planning permission the developers would seed-fund a new stadium. 'Of course the Victorians were gushing with wealth,' he said. 'You're talking about a few key people in the local area building statements and investing in property for the long term. Today there isn't that kind of individual wealth around and they are building for the short term, in truth. Do I see that changing with something like a football stadium? It's a tremendous opportunity to build something that makes a statement ... We've got to make sure we avoid the tin shed scenario.'

Indeed, central Grimsby is full of the hideous tin sheds of retail warehouses. But the Fenty family may not stick around to see the stadium dream through. Having sunk £3 million of his own money into the club already, Fenty would sell to the right buyer. He's already sold his fish business: none of his seven children wanted to take it on. 'They were put off by the long hours,' Fenty said, 'the smelly clothes.'

Before leaving Grimsby I visited another tower, Garibaldi House, one of the ex-council blocks being demolished by Shoreline. As the Dock Tower and the ice factory are emblems of a vanished local capitalism that cared enough about the people to embody its wealth in boastful public buildings, so Garibaldi House is an emblem of that other abdicated local power, the state. Incompetent and indiscriminate as it was in its destruction of old buildings, the postwar, pre-Thatcher state also built decent homes for people who had no other way to get them.

According to Bramley, Shoreline had little choice but to demolish the blocks. It had the money to repair them, but a combination of the desperate poverty of the area and the way the bedroom tax had been designed to favour private land-lords over housing associations and councils meant Shoreline couldn't keep occupancy rates up. Tenants and landlords in East Marsh were in a mirror world. In most of the country, rents on the open market were far higher than the social and 'affordable' rents charged by housing associations. In East Marsh, it was the other way round: the rent you'd pay Shoreline for what used to be a council house was actually the same as, or higher than, rent on the open market. And because, under the bedroom tax, the government wouldn't pay a single tenant's full rent in a two-bedroomed 'social' house, but would happily pay a single tenant's full rent in a two-bedroomed private house, lettings agents had fanned out across the area, encouraging people to move from housing association flats to private ones. If an unemployed working-age woman whose husband had left her moved from a £75 a week two-bedroom Shoreline flat to a £75 a week two-bedroom private flat, she would save £10.50. The consequence of this was to be the permanent destruction of seven hundred well-maintained, not-for-profit homes in a series of controlled demolitions. 'It's not a level playing field,' Bramley said. 'In this area, low-income households are definitely prepared to trade off an extra few pounds in their pocket moving into a low-cost private rented unit against not getting their heating fixed when it breaks down. Cash is king.'

I went to the top of Garibaldi House. The views are supposed to be amazing but it was a murky, hazy day, and the mouth of the estuary was barely visible. I knocked on a few doors. Near the topmost floor I met Denise Gibbs. She was watching an afternoon quiz show on a tiny TV set balanced on top of a small chest, one of the few bits of furniture in her flat. She'd thrown most of the furniture out because it reminded her of her abusive ex-partner. She'd scraped all the wallpaper off the walls for the same reason. She said she'd lived in the flat for thirty years, moved in from the YMCA, lived on the streets before that, had lost her parents when she was a child. Stuck to the bare plaster wall over the TV were two small, faded pictures of Freddie Mercury and Bob Marley, torn from a newspaper. 'I like them,' she said.

'So do I,' I said. She'd had a letter saying the flats were going to be knocked down, and they'd offered her another flat, but she didn't really want to move. 'I did have a carer, but with the government cuts she lost her job. She used to take me out to the big shops. I can't fit in with people, I don't know how to. This is the only home I've ever had.' I asked her who the agency was that had stopped sending the carer. 'Open Door,' she said. 'I got a letter saying I could pop in.'

I left Gibbs, and left Garibaldi House, and left Grimsby. It wasn't until I returned to London that I realised I never asked her how she was going to vote.

On election day, Melanie Onn won Great Grimsby for Labour with a solid majority, increasing the party's vote share compared to Austin Mitchell five years earlier. Victoria Ayling was beaten into third place by the Conservatives.

Nationally, David Cameron's Conservatives won. The Liberal Democrats they'd reluctantly shared government with for the previous five years were annihilated at the polls. Ukip won a single seat. When Labour appointed as its new leader Jeremy Corbyn, a left-wing backbencher known, as far as he was known at all, for anti-militarism, defending the rights of Palestinians and Irish Republicans, rebelling against his own party and addressing protestors at demonstrations, it seemed to many establishment commentators that Cameron's hold on power was secure.

The manifesto the Tories took to the people in 2015 is a jarring read now. It contains the seemingly unambiguous promise to the voters to 'give you a say over whether we should stay in or leave the EU, with an in-out referendum by the end of 2017'. The promise was kept; the referendum was set for 23 June 2016. But it was less clear-cut than it seemed. In the manifesto, the possibility of a 'leave' vote wasn't allowed for. The referendum pledge was accompanied by columns of detailed policy plans for how, under the Conservatives, Britain would develop its future relationship with the EU, from within, as a member. There was no corresponding detail about its future relationship with the

EU if the country decided to quit. There was nothing about this possibility at all. The voters were promised the opportunity to vote to leave, but weren't given an idea what voting 'leave' meant, and weren't offered a clue as to what a Conservative government would do if 'leave' won a majority.

This was only partly because, taking their cue from Cameron, future cabinet ministers didn't have a clue themselves, although we now know they didn't. The main reason was that the Conservative Party was, and remains, two ideologically coherent parties masquerading as one: the liberal libertarian party of David Cameron and George Osborne, which deemed the EU politically awkward but economically necessary, and the party of traditionalist libertarians like Jacob Rees-Mogg, who saw and still see the EU as the enemy. The former couldn't have put any detail about a plan to leave the EU in the manifesto because that would have implied such an outrageous outcome was possible, and that they'd be responsible for it. The latter had no wish for any detail, because leaving was all that mattered, and any attempt to spell out the 'what' and 'how' risked alerting the voters to the fact that whatever 'leaving' meant, it would be hard and expensive. One Conservative Party cynically offered voters a choice it didn't believe was a choice, while the other, with all the sobriety and responsibility of a student on ketamine, embraced the chance to hurl their country into the unknown.

After Grimsby, I'd wondered about the difference between the disruptive new parties like Ukip and the establishment parties, and how there seemed an unbridgeable gap between powerless disruptors and powerful incumbents. And there was. What I hadn't considered was the possibility that an establishment party would steal the disruptive element from its upstart rival and try to use it without making any allowance for the fact that one faction of the thieves believed it to be poison and the other ambrosia. Many Remainers consider David Cameron the worst prime minister of all time because he enabled Britain's exit from the European Union, against his own wishes and beliefs, when he didn't have to. And yet it would have been perfectly possible to make a reasonable case for Britain leaving the EU, and to come up with a sound, twenty-year programme for leaving it. If David Cameron is Britain's worst prime minister, it's because he promised voters they could trigger a staggering disruption – tearing the country from an institution its fabric had been woven with for two generations – when he had no plan to manage the effects of that disruption, and when his party was inherently incapable of coming up with one.

As the referendum approached, although the polls suggested a narrow Remain victory, I began to wonder what leaving might look like in practice, and what those who'd be most affected imagined it would look like. Some of the strongest Eurosceptics were farmers. And yet farmers were among the biggest beneficiaries of EU membership, their livelihoods bound up with EU subsidies and tariffs. When Britain joined the EU's precursor organisation, much of the debate, when it wasn't about fish, was about farmed food. How did the prospect of leaving look from the countryside now?

2

Leaving the Land and Remaining

Norfolk 2016

We perceive the countryside as if farmed fields were the default state, as if 'land' and 'fields' were synonymous. But why should this be, when so much else has changed? To the traveller passing at speed, even to the hiker or dog-walker, farmed fields are anonymous elements that contribute to a pattern. It's the landscape the eye seeks, not any of the fields making it up. Most fields have no individuality to a stranger; at best, a fine oak in the middle, or a pretty horse grazing. Few can tell crops apart, or estimate a field's size in acres. Visitors to the countryside see farms without seeing them. They see the odd farmyard, and they see a mass of fields. A passer-by can't connect a field to a particular farm.

Besides, in Britain, a walk in the country is a constrained experience. Most fields – that is, most bits of the lowland countryside – are forbidden to outsiders, by legal, physical and practical barriers. The biggest barrier is purposelessness:

even where a right of way exists, why use it? To walk from one village to another? We have roads and cars for that. Few who live in 'the country' – that is, in villages – stray from metalled roads except along a handful of known paths for ramblers and dog-walkers, often through woods or along waterways. Most of the vast mosaic of fields will never be entered by any human being except the farmer, a trickle of contractors and, once in a while, a government official. Not that such people are often to be seen. Away from the roads, the space between human habitations in lowland Britain has acquired a Marie Celeste quality. It is rare to visit the countryside or travel through it and see someone at work in a field; the occasional tractor, no more.

But the work gets done. The chequered pattern changes colour and texture, season by season. It's surprising that we treat this epic endeavour as if it were both inevitable and eternal. The colliery tunnels have fallen in, the steel furnaces are winking out, the fishing fleets have gone for scrap; Britain's trains are Japanese, its cars German, its clothes from China. And yet Britain still produces three-fifths of its own food. Farmers still raise livestock, plough fields, sow and harvest crops, at the mercy of the weather. They use technology unrecognisable to their forefathers, but the deep processes go back to the Stone Age and the first farmers. How is this possible? How have so many thriving practices fallen to the globalisation formula of 'other countries do what you do better/more cheaply, so you might as well give up,' while farming, an activity thousands of years old, continues to have mastery of the British lowlands, at a time when the world is awash with cheap (at least for rich countries) food?

Subsidies helped, as did a market of 500 million people protected by high tariffs from global competition. The European Union had been good to farmers. But what if Britain left?

In 1973, when Britain entered the European Economic Community, the forerunner of the EU, everyone older than their early twenties could remember food rationing, and the government's priority was affordable, reliable food supplies. Farmers, accordingly, were subsidised by British taxpayers, but food from abroad could be imported duty-free. Once inside the EEC, a golden age for farm incomes began. Not only were British farmers plugged into the bountiful subsidies of the Common Agricultural Policy, which paid them on the nail for whatever milk, meat and grain they grew, whether there was demand for it or not; they were also sheltered by Europe's tariff barriers. Although they had to compete tariff-free with their fellow European farmers, they were protected from full-on global competition.

The CAP isn't quite so generous today. In the latest version, subsidies aren't based on how much farmers produce, but on how much farmland they own, and payments to the biggest farmers – companies and wealthy landowners – have been trimmed by 5 per cent. It still gives out a lot of money. In 2015, British farmers received slightly more than £3 billion. Outside the EU, subsidies to farmers become just another item in the national budget. They could be increased. They could be kept at the same level. They could be cut. Or a future government could choose to abolish them, as the radical free marketeers of David Lange's Labour Party did when they came to power in New Zealand in the 1980s.

Many British farmers supported Brexit. Others feared it would destroy them. Before the vote the National Farmers

Union came out against, arguing that without subsidies, most British farms would go under. The leaders of the campaign to leave the EU contradicted one another. Some, like the Ukip farming spokesman, Stuart Agnew, and the Conservative farming minister, George Eustice, insisted that, post-Brexit, domestic subsidies would continue to flow, and might even increase. Yet the official campaign, Vote Leave, hinted it was ready to sacrifice farmers to contrive a bonus from Brexit for the country as a whole.

Vote Leave's first campaign poster declared, 'Let's give our NHS the £350 million the EU takes every week.' To understand the significance of this it's first necessary to be clear that the oft-repeated £350 million figure is a lie. Not an exaggeration, or a question of interpretation, or a misleading claim, but a lie. It ignores the rebate Margaret Thatcher negotiated. When you factor that in, the EU actually 'takes' about £250 million a week from Britain. Deepening the dishonesty of the original lie, even that figure overstates Britain's contribution by more than half, because the EU gives much of the country's membership fee straight back. Subsidies to British farmers make up the biggest element of the money that's returned, at £61 million a week.

A more accurate version of the Vote Leave poster would have run: 'Let's abolish farm subsidies, raise taxes and use all the money we save by leaving the EU so we can spend an extra £350 million a week on the NHS.' Wordy, but, for a lot of left-leaning Britons, an attractive plan. Throw in the promise of cheaper food if we dropped tariffs on agricultural imports from Africa, Australasia and the Americas, and it would have been better still. Just not for farmers. There was, after all, another, truthful version of the Vote Leave slogan:

'Let's give our NHS the £61 million our farmers take every week.'

In *The Lost Village*, about life in Pitton in Wiltshire in the 1920s and 1930s, Ralph Whitlock describes the effect on British farming in 1875 of the sudden arrival of ships carrying cheap grain and frozen meat from Latin America, Australia, New Zealand and South Africa. Prices collapsed, and the seemingly eternal patchwork of fields began to fray:

> The marginal land ... was abandoned first, and that included the chalk downlands, large acreages of which had been laboriously brought into cultivation in the years of prosperity. They included most of the downs to the north of Pitton. In the 1920s the villagers were aware of them as miles of dereliction, just over the horizon. It was possible to see the outlines of the deserted fields and even of the plough ridges, for they had been abandoned without even being sown to grass. On some the dominant vegetation was not even weeds but brown and grey lichen ... 1875–93 were the worst years. Thousands of efficient farmers, trying to carry on farming in the well-tried tradition, went bankrupt. Landowners, despairing of finding tenants for their neglected acres, jettisoned vast areas of farmland.

I drove to visit Stuart Agnew one May morning in 2016, seven weeks before the referendum. He was an MEP, but also a farmer, with just over four hundred acres on two parcels of land a couple of miles apart on the sandy soil of north Norfolk, near the market town of Fakenham. Agnew's was a mixed farm, with sheep and chickens as well as crops. It was a measure of how conditions had changed that in the 1970s, his acreage would have been ample for an arable farmer (that is, one growing only crops) to flourish. These days an arable farmer needs a thousand acres – a landholding whose perimeter would take about an hour and a half to walk – to be sure of a decent living in East Anglia.

I was living in Norwich at the time. Google Maps took me west out of the city on a fast road screened by trees from the countryside and ushered me into the dense latticework of lanes on either side of the highway. It was hard to get a sense of the land beyond the hedgerows and woods and shaggy verges, but every so often the hedges would disappear and the landscape would reveal itself, the familiar swell and hollow, the individual fields without meaning because I was travelling past them at fifty miles an hour, because they were like other fields, because they had no grandeur in themselves and were just part of the gentle sweep of the ground towards the sky.

To its farmer, a field is a named enclosure with specific quirks and history and chemistry, an object of husbandry, an almanac of work done and work to do, and an item of account. The subsidy each one brings can be critical to a farm's survival. A typical field under wheat in East Anglia might spread over ten hectares, or twenty-four acres. In a good year in Norfolk you could hope to get eighty-five tonnes of wheat out of a field that size, which would probably be used for animal feed. While eighty-five tonnes might sound like a lot, a tonne of wheat for delivery after the 2016 harvest was selling for just £111. The entire field would yield the farmer £9,435. Against that, set the cost of the seed, fertiliser, sprays and fuel for the tractor that does the spraying, plus a share of the cost of the farm equipment, plus a share of the rent to the landowner or loan payments to the bank, plus a share of a myriad other costs – contractors' fees, fencing, building maintenance, ditching. Only after that is there anything left for the farmer's personal and family needs.

The subsidy was salvation. That same field yielded just over £1,800 in CAP subsidy, almost a fifth of the crop's value. And although the subsidy fluctuated with the exchange rate – it was fixed in euros, but paid in pounds – it was more stable and reliable than the price of wheat, which, in the past nine years, has twice doubled and twice halved, sometimes from one year to the next.

After he became a Ukip MEP in 2009 Agnew relinquished day to day running of the farm to his wife, Diana, who dealt with their 35,000 chickens, and his son Jethro, who tended their seven hundred breeding ewes. The livestock were concentrated on the smaller, northern part of the farm, on the hundred acres Agnew actually owned, up against the former RAF airfield of West Raynham. The rest of the land he farmed as a tenant. Under CAP, farmers got the subsidy either way, as landowners or tenants, as long as they were 'active farmers'. In 2015, Agnew got about £40,000.

The family lived and worked out of a large red brick house, built by Agnew. Around the house, coming right up to it, was sheep pasture, cropped and green as a golf course; close to the front door two ewes suffering crises of maternity were corralled in phonebox-sized wire pens. The newness of it all was signified by the immaturity of the saplings lining the drive to the house and the lack of natural shelter for the sheep.

Set further back from the road was the chicken shed. The hens were free range, which meant that at certain times they are able to come and go between the shed and an outdoor area. Conditions inside the shed at night, when the hens were confined, had been secretly filmed earlier that year by a local animal welfare organisation; the cameraman's film, reported by the *Mail on Sunday*, showed a vast crowd of jostling, scraggly birds, although a subsequent inspection by the RSPCA concluded that, apart from an outbreak of enteritis, which was being treated, the birds were fine.

Further on still was the former airfield, transformed into Britain's largest solar farm, covered in rank after rank of inclined brown panels. Agnew had cut a deal to let his sheep graze underneath them. Since there was also a plan to sow wild flowers around the panels, and since those flower patches might include ragwort, which is poisonous to sheep, Agnew had to divide the solar area into flower paddocks and sheep paddocks. Then he was told that, since the land had been a defence base, 'whenever they sink a fence post, we have to get a bomb disposal expert in to check for unexploded ordnance. We are living in an age now where everything has to be wrapped in cotton wool.'

Agnew was a tall, powerfully built, garrulous man in his mid-sixties. A pupil at Gordonstoun at the same time as Prince Charles, cousin to a baronet with a large estate in Suffolk, he combined a confident, commanding air and the love of a good story with a peevish ability to articulate complaints in a way that aligned his personal disadvantage with the disadvantage to the country. I asked him what would happen if, post-Brexit, farm subsidies were scrapped, and tariffs on imported food cut. 'It would look like a lot of land not being farmed,' he said. 'People being laid off, and a worker would then be on benefits. A farmer who had been making money and paying tax would be wanting a tax refund.' Just as fracking for shale gas should be encouraged to make Britain self-sufficient in energy, he said, British farmers needed to be supported to grow grain, because the country's grain-importing ports were vulnerable to terrorist attack. It was clear he didn't take the prospect of an end to farm subsidies very seriously. He felt that, if anything, EU subsidies weren't high enough. Many countries, he pointed out, subsidised their farmers more generously.

As we talked I realised he was treating the referendum as if it were a general election; as if, instead of resolving a single issue, whether or not to stay in the EU, a vote to leave would usher in a new Britain, where farmer-hampering officials, Agnew-unfriendly regulations, scientists whose analysis he disagreed with and popular hostility to genetically modified food would fade away of their own accord.

He blamed the EU for forcing him to bury sheep rather than cremating them. He blamed the EU for stopping him growing GM crops (he was one of England's trial growers). He blamed the EU for excessively tight control of pesticides and for forcing him to place an electronic tag in the ear of each sheep. 'The trouble is it can fall out. Then it's difficult to know what to replace it with,' he said. 'They say "This animal does not exist" and we say "Well, there it is, defecating and urinating on the concrete."'

I suggested British national bureaucracy, British politicians and British public opinion were capable of banning GM crops and coming up with clumsy hi-tech ways to track sheep without help from Brussels. He wasn't convinced. And although I went to see him to talk about Brexit and farming, because he wanted to leave the EU and was a farmer, we weren't really talking about farming.

We sat in his kitchen, lit by bright daylight from big picture windows. He had a cold and drank from a pint glass of amber liquid – juice or some remedy. I'd read that he'd spent time in Rhodesia and asked him about it and he was off, reminiscing, for an hour. He worked in Rhodesia in the 1970s as a young soil scientist trying to stop earth on white-owned farms being washed away by the rain. He became fond of the country, then run by Ian Smith's white minority government in defiance of the rest of the world, including its former colonial master, Britain, and considered Smith's Rhodesia a great agricultural success story. By that time the war between black nationalist fighters seeking majority rule ('terrorists', Agnew called them) and the white-led regime was well under way. Agnew was sufficiently inspired by the Rhodesian cause to join the country's army, but failed to make it through officer training. He came back to England when he realised Rhodesia was doomed and a black major-ity-ruled Zimbabwe was going to replace it.

'I wouldn't have joined the Tories because of what they did to Rhodesia. That was an absolute betrayal,' he said. He still viewed that time through an inner prism giving a high-contrast spectrum of racial and political categories: the cruel, ruthless 'terrorists'; the non-combatant blacks – he called them 'Africans' – whom he reckoned weren't ready for the responsibility of running the country; the black middle class Smith was apparently trying to foster; the paternalistic British-descended white farmers who paid their black work-ers partly in money, partly in food; the harsh Afrikaner farmers who chained their black workers up; the even less pleasant Portuguese.

Of all his Rhodesia memories he was most energised by the story of a training course he went on with other soil scientists, some of whom were, for the first time, black. He described the mounting apprehension among the white students as the lunch hour approached, their fear that the black students would expect to join them for lunch, that the white students might be forced to go to a multiracial restaurant, or would feel obliged to try to get their colleagues into a whites-only restaurant, where there would be a scene; he described the joy and relief when the black students reassured them, without being asked, that they would find their own place to eat. The black students' acceptance of their status, Agnew said, 'started a better bonding process'.

When we got back to 2016, Agnew talked about immigration. About immigrants from Eastern Europe disrupting the orderly running of schools and hospitals in Lincolnshire 'by sheer force of numbers'. About farms needing cheap Eastern European labour, so EU immigrants already in Britain shouldn't be sent back, but should be closely observed for five years, and deported if they misbehaved. It was as if in his dreaming an empire of strictly enforced castes and races, with white British at the top, was eternally present, only demanding disinterment.

I asked Agnew if there wasn't something quite Ukippy about the EU itself. Couldn't Europe be seen, like the Ukip vision of Britain, as a them and us proposition, an exclusive club that wanted to limit access, to keep out undesirables and prevent its unique character being spoiled? On a world scale, couldn't he consider Europe as an entity cohesive enough, homogeneous enough, to be local?

'I would have been happy with that if it were the Netherlands, Denmark, Scandinavia, perhaps France,' he said, with sudden intensity of feeling. 'I thought that was what it was all about. All these Eastern European countries . . . to try and say "That's us" is very difficult.'

A patina of ancient power, the kind of power that comes with landed wealth and bonds of marriage and mateyness within an exclusive social group, lies over north Norfolk. Eleven miles to the north of Agnew's house was Holkham Hall, where Thomas Coke, Earl of Leicester, still owned farmland on the scale of his eponymous Georgian ancestor, the agricultural reformer Coke of Norfolk. In 2015 the Holkham Farming Company received £183,000 in subsidies; another Holkham enterprise, Holkham Nature Reserve Ltd, run jointly with Natural England (conservation organisations are some of the biggest recipients of farm subsidies) got £205,000. Ten miles to the west of Agnew's house lay the Sandringham Estate, the queen's farm, subsidised to the tune of about £650,000. Between Agnew's place and Sandringham was Houghton Hall, family seat of Robert Walpole, Britain's first prime minister, now the home of David, seventh Marquess of Cholmondeley, Lord Great Chamberlain and beneficiary of £260,000 in subsidies.

The land Agnew's house stood on had been part, until relatively recently, of Marquess Townshend's Raynham Estate. The Townshend family still owned the airfield; the solar farm, one of a string around the UK owned by a specialist investment fund, paid rent to the estate. In its heyday the estate had forty thousand acres. By 2016 it had shrunk to five thousand, although that was enough to bring the Townshends a subsidy of £360,000.

All families are old, but there was something unusually persistent about the Townshends. The family came up in written records as farming land around the various hamlets carrying the Raynham name as early as the fourteenth century, and they had a lock on the area by the mid-sixteenth. The marquess in referendum-tide, Charles Townshend, lived in the proto-Palladian mansion, Raynham Hall, his great-great-great-great-great-great-great-great-grandfather built almost four hundred years ago.

I went to see him one morning, driving through the private park to the house and being shown in by a cleaner in housecoat and rubber gloves to a vast chequerboard-tiled hall: the wrong entrance, I think – I'd been expected round the other side. Lord Townshend, seventy, bearded and a little tired-looking, wearing a body-warmer, blue cords, blue socks and moccasins, took me to a narrow scullery and made me a cup of instant coffee in a delicate teacup, apologising that the household was between butlers. 'He was six foot three,' he said of the previous incumbent. 'He was tall enough to reach the windows.'

We went to the library, lined with eighteenth- and seventeenth-century volumes and with a fine antique twentieth-century electric heater in the fireplace. Lord Townshend showed me a beloved possession, an ivory-handled seal his ancestor Viscount 'Turnip' Townshend had used to endorse the Treaty of Union between England and Scotland in 1706. Besides being Walpole's neighbour and brother-in-law, the viscount was Walpole's partner in government. He was foreign secretary when Britain had two of them, one for Protestant countries and another for Catholic and Muslim ones (Townshend's was the northern department). Then he fell out with Walpole, retreated to his estate and devoted himself to farming so successfully (hence the nickname: he proselytised for turnips) that in popular history Raynham competes with Coke's Holkham to be considered the birth-place of the British agricultural revolution.

It was an awkward meeting. Lord Townshend agreed to see me after a personal introduction, and I thought I'd explained in advance who I was and what I was writing about, but it turned out he believed I was writing a historical piece about agriculture. He'd hoped he might be able to sell me some time in Raynham's archive of 2.5 million docu-ments, which he's trying to catalogue and commercialise. When he learned I was writing about the EU referendum, he said he didn't want to comment. When his discovery that I'd written about privatisation came in close proximity to my questions about the reasons the Raynham Estate had decided to farm its land directly, rather than through tenants, the framework of courtesy on which my presence in his house depended began to stretch and creak like the stays of a rope bridge in a high wind. It's not that he was angry, but he seemed to fear I wished him ill, and it was too late to explain that even if I'd wanted to I couldn't blame him for the enclo-sures, the flight from the land to the cities and the disappear-ance of the English peasantry.

His son, Lord Townshend said, ran the farming side. Having inherited the title and the estate late in life, just before his sixty-fifth birthday, he was focused on the house, which a senior historian at English Heritage had called the most beautiful in England. 'I'm restoring Raynham Hall and bringing it into the twenty-first century. My second interest is keeping the family and the estate together.' This wasn't easy, he explained. 'The house doesn't lend itself to being open to the public. We've not got great wings or basements where the family can live as at Houghton or Holkham. They were built as showcases for the plunder of the Grand Tours. This house was built as a home, as a private house.' That said, there are recitals, and anyone can arrange a tour, if they can get together a party of fourteen, at £30 a head.

When aristocrats own so much land, when all the peers I've mentioned, out of the thousands of possibilities, attended the same secondary school, the one attended by David Cameron and Boris Johnson, it might seem strange to say that the powers of the lords of Norfolk have waned. But in some senses they have. They no longer wield local power over hundreds of tenants and agricultural workers and their families on their estates; commuters, retirees and second-homers live in the villages now. Nor do they have the wider power their status once gave them in the armed forces of the Empire and in Parliament, reaching out from the manor to the world.* Lord Townshend inherited his title just after the automatic right of hereditary peers to sit in the House of Lords was abolished. In British national politics the dialectics of inequality are central, but in the politics of localism, nationalism and globalism, the politics of the EU referendum, a different dynamic comes into play. In terms of the

---

* One of Turnip Townshend's grandsons, as chancellor of the Exchequer, came up with the idea of raising money for Britain by taxing tea in the American colonies.

citizen-Westminster-Brussels arc, it was less significant that the Townshends had a big house and thousands of acres of land, when so many had no house and no land, than that when I called Raynham Hall, Lord Townshend answered the phone. In an economy of faceless authorities and absentee landlords, he was present, and had a face.

Still, in an age of austerity, £360,000 a year is a lot of public dosh to take to the bank when one of your concerns is finding a new butler. I asked Lord Townshend about the scenario where, post-Brexit, farm subsidies were slashed, and farmers deserted the land en masse. 'The idea that a loss of subsidies would lead to the dereliction of the countryside is defeatist,' he said. 'I just feel we have been, throughout history, able to get through any problem thrown at us by politics, and I don't see why we shouldn't be able to continue to do it. I've enough confidence in our abilities to survive in England, based on our history, that we will do the right thing if subsidies disappear. We will still survive. And farm.'

After I left Raynham Hall I got lost in the lanes and the fields. Google Maps will lead you into the depths of the Norfolk countryside until the signal is too poor for you to be led back. I pulled over to get my bearings and an agricultural vehicle squeezed past, ten times the size of my car, sprouting prongs and blades, like a rover sent from another planet to explore the earth. When it had gone all was silent except for the sound of two wild stags banging their heads together at the edge of a field a few yards away, under the yellow spring oak leaves.

The Townshends got back the freehold of West Raynham airfield after it closed in the 1990s, but the houses where

RAF personnel and their families lived were bought by a property developer who went spectacularly bust after the crash, owing a South African bank £20 million. Of 172 homes in what became a new village known as the Kiptons, many have been let or sold. The topography of rank is preserved: big detached and semi-detached officers' houses in Kipton Orchard, terraced houses where airmen and their families lived in Kipton Wood. The promised gym, swimming pool and church never materialised, and there was no school or doctor's surgery, but residents said things had got better since the bank called in its loan to the developer and took on the responsibility of refurbishing homes and common spaces. There was a bus service. When I visited Kipton Wood, the grass in front of the severe, solid, red brick terraces was neatly cut, and the children had a playground. The community shop, which doubles as a pub two nights a week, was open, waiting for a delivery of eggs from Diana Agnew.

'Before the shop and pub were open we were bored seven nights out of seven and now we've got a darts team going. Got a proper community feel,' said Zara England, a shop volunteer. 'Four and a half years ago nobody spoke to anybody, the shop was privately run so you couldn't afford to shop here anyway.'

Peter Harris, another volunteer, was one of the first to move in, from his native Fakenham, in 2008. His career as a road engineer had been cut short when he slipped while carrying a 75kg kerbstone and badly injured his back. He hasn't worked since. Money was tight and the developer offered him a low rent on a shell of a house with holes in the roof, telling him he was welcome to fix it himself. The move appealed to his wife, who'd lived on the active base as a little girl, when her father was a radar specialist servicing anti-aircraft missiles. When I met him the Harrises had two small children; he was in pain, on medication and hard to employ, while his wife had completed an Open University degree and was training to be a teacher.

I asked about the referendum. Harris said he didn't feel he had enough information.

Zara England brought up immigration, though not in the way I'd got used to. 'The people who want to come out are pushing the race card, which I think is bang out of order,' she said. 'Polish workers work a damn sight harder than the English. People can whinge about how they can't get a job because Polish Jim has got it, but would they flip burgers eight hours a day?' She used to work for Burger King.

'We don't get much diversity round here,' she said. 'Ninety-five per cent of the children are white and of that probably 60 per cent are blonde.'

'Back in the 1980s,' Harris mused, 'there was one black person in Fakenham and everybody knew him. Lovely chap. Now half the time you can walk the streets of the town and hear people speaking languages . . . you think you're on holiday.

'I guarantee you about 20 per cent of the people here will vote. People feel they're screwed either way.'

When I'd spoken to Agnew about farm work, he'd described a kind of apartheid, where aboriginal Brits had come to think of field labour as 'immigrant work', and Eastern European gangmasters would only hire Eastern Europeans. That wasn't quite the way Harris put it when he talked about his own early experience of farming. He just thought the farmers were mean. 'I did two weeks on an organic farm when I was sixteen . . . You have to go through taking all the weeds out, taking all the stones out. Picking up carrots out of the ground. As a kid of sixteen you see yourself doing much better. If the farmers had paid better, I would have stayed.'

In a sense the people of the Kiptons lived in the country, and in a sense they didn't. Like many villages, marooned in private open space, the Kiptons lacked open space that was public. It was surrounded by fields, but didn't have a park of its own, or a field for community events. The feeling of living on a military base with a secure perimeter had been carried over from RAF days – people talked about 'going off-site' – and there was no connection between the community and farming. There was even a clause in the tenancy agreements forbidding the keeping of farm animals. Although it was two and a half hours from London, one of Harris's neighbours was a shift commuter: four days in the capital, four days in Norfolk. All the people of the Kiptons saw of farmers was the tractor the bus got stuck behind on the way to Fakenham.

'You feel separate from them but at the same time you feel they are around you,' Harris said. 'You hear machinery most days in the fields. The sound of a shotgun. You can definitely smell the chicken mess when it comes across the fields.'

I found a hierarchy of security even among farmers working relatively large farms. The most secure were the landowner-farmers, like the Townshend family or the big companies growing fruit and vegetables over thousands of acres in Lincolnshire and Cambridgeshire. Next came farmers with long-term tenancies, like Stuart Agnew, who could still call a farm their own, even if they didn't own the land. Finally there were contractor farmers: farm managers and workers hired job by job, season by season, who took a wage to work land for somebody else. To make the leap from contractor to fully fledged farmer took backing, or an inheritance. Farms big in acreage could still be very small businesses in terms of employees, and they were often family businesses. One of the great generators of unhappiness in the countryside had nothing to do with politics and everything to do with generations: some farmers had farms to hand on to children who didn't want to farm them, while others refused to step aside to make way for children who were desperate to take over. If farm subsidies did take a hit, and farms became fewer, it wouldn't be because of a shortage of people who wanted to farm.

Some had seen their patrimony disintegrate before they had a chance to inherit it. James Lake did. His grandfather started a mushroom-growing business in Hertfordshire and moved it to Little Fransham in Norfolk, a few miles south of the Agnew and Townshend farms and the old airfield, in the 1960s. By the time Lake was born in the 1970s the family had fourteen temperature-controlled growing sheds on three acres of concrete. They made their own growing medium out of a mixture of chicken manure and horse manure from Newmarket racing stables, then mixed that with mushroom spore-impregnated grain. 'Put it in growing boxes, which would go into the growing shed, and six weeks later you would have mushrooms. All picked by hand. We had gangs of women, mainly. Blokes weren't dextrous enough.' That kind of farming got few subsidies in Britain but mushrooms were a luxury product in those days and the Lakes prospered. They employed thirty-five people. They began to export.

Lake maintains that his family's farm fell victim to unfair practices. In the mid-1990s, Irish competitors – 'they got a lot of European funding to basically sort themselves out' – started supplying British supermarket chains with cheap mushrooms wholesale.

'The supermarkets would say "We'd love to buy UK mushrooms but you're going to have to do it at that price,"' Lake said. British mushroom growers started going out of business. Their Dutch counterparts were suffering too. They reacted by buying ailing British mushroom firms, trucking in their own product and packaging it here, enabling the supermarkets to take advantage of ambiguous EU origin labelling rules to stick Union Jacks on the packaging. 'Dad went down to Westminster with a few of the growers,' Lake said. '[The politicians] just sat there and said "I can't imagine the supermarkets would do anything like that."'

They shut down in 2002, after trying to diversify their way out. 'We looked at all different ideas, from going upmarket to growing more exotic strains and pre-sliced. We even looked at grow-your-own kits. We were getting 90p for a pound of mushrooms. We could just about pick them for that price but we couldn't put them on a lorry and deliver them so we were getting more and more into debt. Also there was a virus going round, virus X. We got the start of that. We had to shut the farm down, empty everything out, sterilise it. We said "Enough is enough." The year we closed twelve other mushroom farms of similar size or larger went under.'

The Lakes were comparatively lucky. After giving up their mushroom business they got permission to use the land to plant the most valuable crop of all: houses. They cleared their debts with a little left over. By 2016, after various different jobs, Lake was a contractor, driving agricultural machinery for other people, wanting a farm of his own but not seeing how he could get one. To start a viable farm from scratch, he reckoned, would cost a million pounds. 'However much I want to have my own farm, I don't think I would want the stress and hassle of having to borrow that much money.'

He spoke in the big sitting room of his house, a house built with mushroom money in the good times. I'd arranged to come over after eight in the evening because that was the earliest he could manage. He'd already cancelled one meeting over farm work. A few days earlier he'd started work at six a.m., spraying, then gone combining at lunchtime and carried on till 3.30 a.m. the next day, working by the combine harvester's headlights.

Theoretically, a withdrawal of subsidies for British farmers could open up new opportunities as the price of farmland fell and existing farmers sold up. But most of the insiders I spoke to felt it would simply speed up a process that was already under way, of consolidation, of small and medium farms being absorbed by larger ones. 'The bigger farms are getting bigger,' Lake said. 'The days of the small family farm are numbered. Your traditional mixed farm, where you've got land, some cows, some pigs, some sheep, are pretty much over. You have to go big or go home.'

'There's a pretty real risk that if we came out of Europe the level of support for farming would be under pressure,' said Hector Wykes-Sneyd, a Suffolk land agent. 'The results of that would be quite interesting. You will see a lot of land coming out of production. It will also lead to something that's been going on quietly, not necessarily very obviously

– economies of scale, big operators. If you can afford this extremely expensive machinery, if you have the acreage to support it, you can farm huge acreage at low cost. I would see that process continuing.'

The farmer who employed Lake used to farm his seven hundred acres of land with just three and a half people – himself, two workers and a student to help out at harvest time. On the eve of the referendum he still had the seven hundred acres, but on top of that was tenant on another two hundred and fifty, and contract farmed a further seven hundred. His farm had more than doubled in size, yet three and a half people was still plenty to do the job.

Those who couldn't scale up, Wykes-Sneyd said, would suffer. 'If [subsidies] disappeared entirely there would be a lot of farming organisations that wouldn't make a profit. A farmer has this innate desire to keep farming their land and do the best by it to the extent the old belt-tightening exercise is very real. It's amazing how people will get through years where other companies would have folded up. But if you take subsidies out that will not go on very long.'

I remember my school history curriculum bigging up Turnip Townshend and Coke of Norfolk, the great landowner reformers of the eighteenth and nineteenth centuries, who did such clever things, and raised yields, with crop rotation and clover and rationalising peasants off their bitty fragments of the commons. This narrative of the agricultural revolution has come under attack in recent years. The most frequent line of criticism is that the likes of Townshend and Coke weren't innovators, but brilliant publicists and prose-lytisers who worked out how to systemise and promote much older ideas. A fiercer attack came from Robert Allen in 1992 in his book *Enclosure and the Yeoman*. Allen described two English agricultural revolutions, one by small yeoman farmers in the seventeenth century, another by landlords in the eighteenth. The yeomen's revolution, he maintained, led to a big increase in crop yields, with the same amount of labour; the landlords' revolution used less labour to grow the same amount of crops. The earlier revolution, in Allen's view, enriched the country as a whole without mass unemployment; the more celebrated landlords' revolution only benefited the landlords.

Allen's sally, loaded with data as it was, wasn't decisive; Turnip and company have their redoubts in the academy yet. But the bigger point is that we are still on the reforming landlords' vector, of ever larger farms run by ever fewer people, economies of scale, the application of science to the problem of growing food, and the pressure to acquire highly specialised and hence highly expensive machinery. Between 2007 and 2016 inflation was 31 per cent, while the price of a tractor doubled, but for that money you got a tractor that drove itself in a perfectly straight line down a field, guided by GPS. All the farmer had to do was turn it round when it got to the end. The word Wykes-Sneyd used to describe modern farming was 'precise': the precision with which vegetables will be planted in a field, again using GPS, so that they can be harvested by machine without loss; the precision that comes of using the right pesticides and fertilisers, in exactly the right quantity, at exactly the right time.

And those quantities, on a big, conventional British farm, are large: about 250kg of nitrogen, potash and phosphate fertiliser per arable hectare. Lately farmers have been putting increasing amounts of sulphur on their fields to compensate – I know it sounds unlikely – for the essential sulphur they used to receive from acid rain. This kind of mechanised, chemical-intensive, large-scale farming is widespread around the world, wherever farmers can afford fertiliser. Lord Townshend told me how he'd been assured by the Algerian minister of agriculture that 'Turnip Townshend was where we started learning our agricultural procedures.' The principles of the aristo-capitalist agricultural revolution – big farms replacing small ones, maximising food production through science – were followed by twentieth-century socialist progressives.

David Laborde, of the International Food Policy Research Institute, pointed out to me that this kind of farming rendered absurd notions of food self-sufficiency for Britain, or even Europe. Britain grew three-fifths of its own food but had no phosphate reserves. Nor did any other EU country. The nearest phosphate was in Morocco.

I'd approached Laborde with two questions I thought were straightforward. One was about what 'cheap imported food' actually meant today. With oil, it's easy. There's one world price, but the cost of getting the oil out of the ground varies from place to place, mainly according to how difficult it is to get at and how much local workers are paid. It's simple, for any oilfield, to work out how low the world price would have to go to stop oil extraction being profitable.* Saudi oil is cheap; North Sea oil is expensive. How to find similar benchmarks for food?

---

* Actually it isn't simple at all – financial journalists just write about it as if it is. But it's easier than doing the same sums for food.

As I talked to Laborde, I realised how naive my question was. It's not just that the Saudi Arabia of rice, the Saudi Arabia of prawns and the Saudi Arabia of soya beans are all different. It's that with staple crops like wheat, there are multiple different grades, varieties and uses, making it hard to compare like with like. There was a more obvious problem. I was imagining a scenario where Britain no longer subsidised its farmers and simply imported the cheapest food from wherever it was available. I'd forgotten that, just because Britain no longer subsidises its farmers, other countries won't stop subsidising theirs. Some cheap imported food is cheap not because it's grown where it's most rational to grow it, but because it's subsidised. Like the EU, the United States, India and China all subsidise their farmers heavily, as do many smaller countries. And if all subsidies and all tariffs were magically to disappear? 'The production of food in developing countries, especially in Africa but also in Latin America, would start to grow,' Laborde said. 'You would have poor farmers in those countries getting out of poverty.'

This seemed like an answer to my second question. I wanted to know what Britain should do about subsidies to farmers if the wellbeing of the world's 800 million undernourished people were its only concern. Would the risk of British farmland going unfarmed be outweighed by the benefits to the world's poor if subsidies were scrapped after Brexit? Yes, Laborde said; but Britain outside the EU was not a big enough food producer to tip the scales of global dearth and plenty one way or the other.

And if, as predicted, the world population peaked at ten billion – could the planet support that many mouths? Again, the answer was yes, but a more nuanced yes. The issue, he said, was not so much whether enough food could be grown – it could – as whether the poor would be able to afford it. To understand what he was talking about, you have to look at another, more recent agricultural revolution.

In the early 1980s, British farming encountered an unexpected crisis. Propelled towards prosperity and a sense of their own success by generous European subsidies, ever more ingenious scientific techniques and an agriculture ministry still fixated on the idea that its only aim was to maximise and streamline the production of food, farmers lost the trust of the British people. As the old CAP subsidy regime generated grain mountains and lakes of surplus milk, it began to dawn on the non-farming population that the drive for yield to the exclusion of all else was altering the appearance of the countryside in a way they didn't like. Each year, ten thousand miles of hedgerow were being dug up. In eastern England, up to 90 per cent of trees at field boundaries had been felled to create space for bigger fields and the manoeuvring of new, bigger machinery. Conservationists were beginning to note the waning of familiar British species; hedge destruction, monoculture and pesticides meant that increasingly they had nowhere to live, and nothing to eat. Friends of the Earth began peaceful direct action against farmers. Farmers burned conservationists in effigy. In her 1980 polemic, *The Theft of the Countryside*, Marion Shoard unsparingly articulated the alienation, as she saw it, between farmers and the people as a whole: she called them 'executioners' carrying out a death sentence on the English landscape, turning it into 'a vast, featureless expanse of prairie'.

Matters came to a head one weekend in June 1984 when a single Norfolk farmer, David Archer, provoked turmoil at the top of the government. Archer had a farm in the Halvergate Marshes on the Norfolk Broads, an area of wetland grazing between Norwich and the sea where for centuries domestic cattle, wild birds and wild flowers have co-existed. In the early 1980s farmers, with the support of the Ministry of Agriculture, began to press to drain the land and plant crops on it. *The Times* called Halvergate 'the Flanders of the great war between farming interests and the objectives of nature conservation'. The government tried to persuade the farmers to stop voluntarily while it worked out what to do.

On Thursday, 21 June, Archer told civil servants he was opting out of their voluntary scheme, and that, the next Monday, he was going to start draining the land for ploughing. The only way he could be stopped was by a direct order from Patrick Jenkin, the environment secretary. Cabinet papers released recently show a furious squabble between Jenkin and his counterpart at the Ministry of Agriculture, Michael Jopling. Jenkin wanted to make the order, rather than lose part of the 'traditional landscape in the Broads' and face the 'outcry from the conservationists'. Jopling accused him of panicking and of threatening the customary Tory defence of private property. Thatcher intervened on Jenkin's side over the weekend; the order was made, and Archer was forced to stay his ditching gear. But the fundamental problem had become too vexatious for its resolution to be postponed. How to make farmers respect the needs of conservation without standing in the way of their need to grow food and desire to make money? How to reconcile a public good

– the beauty of the countryside, the sound of birdsong – with the fact that the farmers had both legal and customary occupation of the space in which these public goods were supposed to be maintained?

As far back as 1969, there'd been a recognition that demonising farmers wasn't the only way to go. At the Silsoe Exercise in Hertfordshire, farmers and conservationists tried working together on an actual farm. An idea began to emerge that, rather than trying to subjugate farmers to conservation, farmers might become conservationists. After all, they were already on the government payroll; why not simply tinker with the contract? A new set of organisations, the Farming and Wildlife Groups, or FWAGs, appeared as interpreters between the two hostile cultures. Fifteen years later, when the government needed to resolve the conflict on the Broads, a set of principles already existed.

In 1985, the government set up the Broads Grazing Marshes Conservation Scheme. The name was cumbersome, the location obscure, but it was the start of a new revolution in European agriculture. Up till then the only way governments had found to slow the rush to ever more intensive farming was to pay farmers compensation for not doing something they would otherwise have done. Farmers got subsidies for farming, or subsidies for not farming. This was different. Farmers who signed up to the scheme were given an extra subsidy on top of the old one for farming according to a detailed programme drawn up with wildlife experts. They were expected to limit the number of animals they grazed, cut hay no more than once a year and restrict pesticide use. For the first time, farmers were being paid by the state to do something other than maximise food output or slam on the brakes to stop over-production. They were being paid to be farmer-conservationists: a formalisation of a role farmers always thought they had anyway, that of stewards of the land.

At first, the European Commission and other national governments were baffled by and suspicious of what John Sheail, in his history of British environmentalism, calls 'the concept of making payments to farmers to farm below the maximum'. There were mutterings that it was illegal. But the commission came round, and Europe took up the concept. For the first time, member states could subsidise farmers to provide a public good as well as to grow food. Farmers were contracted not only to protect the aesthetic value of the countryside and wildlife habitats but to increase recreational access to their land for the public.

In the beginning, in Britain, the practice was confined to famously pretty and fragile farmed landscapes like the Broads, the Cotswolds, the Lake District, Shetland and Loch Lomond, which were designated Environmentally Sensitive Areas. Thirty years later, farmers anywhere who are prepared to adhere to complex, rigid, tightly inspected regimes of conservation and access on their land – regimes that will diminish their food production – can earn handsome sums on top of their regular subsidies by becoming stewards of the countryside.

More significantly, the idea has been embedded in the CAP itself. The farm subsidy system has two parts. The first is what non-farmers understand by 'farm subsidies': direct payments to help farmers farm, based on acreage, known as Pillar 1. The second element, Pillar 2, is for what's vaguely known as 'rural development', which covers everything from preserving traditional farming practices and preventing the depopulation of the countryside to conservation and public access. Stewardship payments come out of the Pillar 2 pot. But since 2004, farmers getting Pillar 1 payments, the basic subsidy they rely on, have also been obliged to carry out an extensive list of 'cross-compliance' measures, many related to the environment. If they don't – by not leaving wide enough wildlife-friendly borders around their crop fields, for instance – they'll be fined. Since last year, a third of Pillar 1 payments have become tied to an additional set of 'greening measures'. These are decisive steps by the EU towards obliging farmers to become custodians of the countryside. All the figures I've given for farm subsidies up to now include both the greening tithe and Pillar 2 payments. Much of the Holkham Estate subsidy is for conservation, rather than conventional farming; and just under a tenth of Agnew's subsidy last year came from conservation, a proportion he would like to see increase post-Brexit, though he seethes at the requirement to erect an 'EU gratitude plaque' of statutory size.

'If we did nothing we would have a UK that would lose the water vole, that would never see a lapwing,' Heidi Smith, of Norfolk FWAG, told me. 'The turtle dove would go. You would go out on a summer's day and not see any butterflies. Most farmland is drenched in broad spectrum insecticides so there are no insects to be found anywhere. Farming birds are threatened because they have nothing to eat and nowhere to live.' But FWAG has to work with farmers, not against them. 'FWAG is very careful we don't see ourselves as too niche,' she said. 'There is a huge amount they can do without giving up their chemicals.'

I visited Richard Wright, one of FWAG's star clients. He won an award in 2014 for conservation work. He farms a little over four hundred acres on the Broads, halfway between Norwich and the coast, 185 acres of grazing for a herd of 110 beef cattle on the marshes beside the River Yare and the rest arable on the low slopes above. In 2015, according to government records, he got a basic subsidy of £33,265.59, and half as much again from the stewardship package.

He took me up to a place where his barley field met his wheat field and showed me the kinds of thing he had to do to earn his stewardship money. 'The grass strip you see there,' he said, pointing to the edge of the barley field, 'is impregnated with flowers, specially for bees. At the moment the flowers are coming up; in about four or five weeks' time they'll be about that tall, and they'll come out in flower all through the summer into the autumn, so the bees will be able to feed on them.' I looked at the broad strip of uncultivated land running all around the field. Why was it that width? 'We're paid to do a set area. The payment will be compensation for me not having corn on there. We do one metre extra. Just so we're covered. Just to be on the safe side. We can't afford to lose that money.'

He showed me more. The beetle bank, a ridge of soil that encouraged insects and turned into a nesting site for grey partridges; the insects ate aphids that preyed on the crops, which let him reduce his spray use. The bare patches in the fields were for skylarks to nest in. 'Three years ago we'd have seen one, two pairs of skylarks; we're now up to fifteen, twenty pairs. And it's rising all the time. We're contracted to have ten of these skylark plots on the farm. It's what we're paid for. But I've looked at it and said, "Well, actually, if we've got so much success with the skylarks, there's that many more needs nesting sites." We're actually up to like fifteen plots this year. Each year we're putting in a few more extra plots at our own expense.'

He showed me bat runs, linking stretches of hedge for bats to follow, hoovering up insects as they fly along. He showed me an edging strip that looked like a strip of weeds. It was a strip of weeds. Weeds for the flowers, for the bees, for the birds, for the insects. In another field, more weeds; a 'low input' crop of barley planted with 40 per cent less seed, treated with 30 per cent less fertiliser, sprayed not with weed-killer but with weed stunter. The soil was busy with a wild bird seed smorgasbord of kale, linseed and mustard. Long, dry stalks of gold-of-pleasure stuck up sparsely like a bald man's combover come loose. 'Winter time, you come here, clap your hands, there will be flocks, a hundred, a hundred and fifty linnets, goldfinches, skylarks, all manner of birds,' Wright said.

I asked: 'Do you ever have moments when you kind of shake yourself and you think "They're paying me to grow weeds"?' He laughed. 'It's what we're paid to do. But the point is, our aim is to create a mosaic. You cannot just pick the options. Everything is in it together. Birds can come in here and then when they grow up they can nest in here. It'll be ideal for little chicks to run around in. It's low density, it'll give them canopy from predators, but they can move around in here, feed off the insects. Everything is linked.'

Alongside all this, or within it, Wright carried out conventional farming as it's been practised in Britain for generations. The wheat might go for animal or human food, perhaps Weetabix, depending on the quality. I looked at the young green seedlings. How much land did it take to grow one Weetabix? About a foot square, Wright reckoned. The barley was grown for a whisky distillery in the Highlands. Wright's acres would produce enough for 264,000 bottles of Scotch.

He took me through the life of the field: in August, it's harvested, and the stubble is left over the winter. In February, it's ploughed and sown. Once the seed sprouts, the first of two fertiliser applications goes on. I could see the white nodules of fertiliser lying on the top layer of soil. Wright was about to spray the field with herbicide. Later there would be one, possibly two fungicides, and, depending on the verdict of an independent agronomist, a pesticide. What would happen, I asked, if he didn't spray or use artificial fertilisers? 'You'd have a massive infestation of weeds and disease and a massive reduction in crop yield.' And was there anything he'd put on the field if he wasn't constrained by the new rules? 'No restraints whatsoever? I'd put houses on there. I'd make a lot more money.'

Wright's father was a farmer. So was his grandfather, who started working life as a farm labourer in wartime before getting a farm of his own. Wright is likeable, a cheerful, patient fifty-six-year-old, born in the place where he farms. He spoke with real enthusiasm and pride of his conservation work. All the same there was a strain of defensiveness, a sense of injustice, that kept coming through; a feeling that farmers as a class have been and continue to be defamed, and that a retraction was warranted. He criticised organic farmers for making poor single mothers feel bad about not being able to afford their products. He criticised Britain's animal-welfare-motivated ban on intensive pig farmers (he used to be one) as backward. At one point I looked up and saw Wright's Land Rover parked on a ridge under a lone tree, framed and illuminated by the mellow May sunshine, and remarked that it looked like a Land Rover advertisement. It was a throwaway comment, but Wright was quick to tell me his Land Rover was a working farm vehicle, not a luxury car for the school run. I remembered something James Lake had said: 'The image of a farmer here is of tweeds and a Range Rover, whereas in France and Germany a farmer is just a member of society.'

What surprised me was the anger Wright felt towards big conservation organisations, particularly the Royal Society for the Protection of Birds. I'd assumed he'd see himself as at least partly in the same sphere as the charity, given that he was doing so much conservation work; he's a farmer-conservationist, the RSPB are conservationist-farmers (the RSPB is the fourth largest UK recipient of farm subsidies, with almost £7 million last year, not all of it for conservation work). But he didn't. 'The RSPB has just got a million pounds to buy a piece of land further down the valley which they will turn into a nature reserve. They will downgrade the farming there. They've got government funding to buy it, government funding to look after it, they will get all the farm subsidies on it, they've got teams of people who are employed to make sure they get every penny they can – their membership will pay to visit and look at the wildlife on there – they do not want to say "Well, actually farmers are doing conservation." They want to discredit farmers, because their main thing is the income from the public. To keep that going they have to be seen as the only saviours of the countryside.'

I asked if he'd embraced the conservation side of his work, or was sad that he had to do it this way. 'My father isn't happy with this, because he was brought up to produce food,' Wright said. 'I can see the benefits. The birds sing etc. And it does bring in an income. When you've got the price of corn, one year it's £110 a tonne, a few years ago it was £200, the payment we get for [conservation] gives us a little bit of a level income. I've got a family to feed, a mortgage to pay . . . We're not like the big corporate charities who get lottery funding to buy land, government funding, tax relief for being a charity, even though they are becoming a twenty-first-century version of the landed gentry.'

He was grateful for one aspect of his new life: he got to meet people when he talks about his work. Mechanisation has isolated farmers. Wright and his brother farmed alone where once fourteen people worked. 'I can go seven to seven, I will see no one, I will speak to no one,' he said. 'Until we did this and won the award and there was a piece in the paper about it, our standing in the village was rock bottom. We were just farmers who destroy everything. But when the public hear about this, all of a sudden: hey, you're the guy who does that – the butterflies! The birds! And our standing in the village has shot up.'

As I was leaving he told me I'd forgotten to ask a question.

'What?'

'Which way I'm going to vote in the referendum.'

'Which way are you going to vote?' He'd already told me that post-Brexit the fight to control the countryside would intensify.

'Out.'

'Why?'

'It'd be bad for farming, but there are some things more important than farming.'

'What things?' He wouldn't say.

From the summit of Wright's fields, there was a fine view of the Broads, green and glittering and perfectly flat, scored with drainage ditches that surrounded each square of grazing land, and the silos of the Cantley sugar factory on the far side of the Yare. Two thousand years ago, when it was Roman land, and the language of the natives was either Latin or a form of early Welsh, the Broads was tidal, a delta landscape of water and mudflats. The coastline was a mile further out than today. Three wide rivers, the Bure, the Yare and the Waveney, opened out into a great estuary, four miles wide at the mouth, where the seaside resort of Great Yarmouth now stands. The geography of Roman Norfolk can still be seen; the remains of the town of Venta Icenorum lie close to a small, shallow stream, but in its day it was a port for sea-going vessels, which would sail east, past Wright's farm – his arable fields would have been the right bank of the river – and out through the Great Estuary to the North Sea, between the Roman fortifications of Caister and Burgh Castle, whose flint ramparts are still there.

It's uncertain how much climate change had to do with the collapse of Roman Britain and the subsequent settlement, or conquest, or trickle-in, of the Angles and the Saxons, or how far climate change was responsible for the silting up of the estuary that transformed the landscape and eventually created the Broads. What we do know is that the landscape was transformed. It's one of the moments in history that the deniers of human-induced climate change cling to – look, climate changes all the time, it's not us! – but the disappearance of the estuary within recorded history is a salutary reminder of the impermanence of land and the folly of destabilising, as we are doing, an already unstable climate. Farmer-conservationists like Wright have moved a long way from their old mindset, but according to some radical farmers, when global warming is the peril, they haven't moved nearly far enough.

One such was Peter Melchett, the former head of Greenpeace UK, who owned the 890-acre Courtyard Farm in northwest Norfolk, near Hunstanton. He was also a hereditary peer, also an Etonian, also in receipt of a six-figure subsidy (£107,545 last year). But he was the only member of the Norfolk farming aristocracy to have spent two nights in a Norwich jail, in 2000, for attempting to purge a local farmer's field of an experimental crop of GM maize.* Like Wright, Melchett was a farmer–conservationist, and rewarded for it by the subsidy system. Unlike Wright, he was an organic farmer; he was the policy director of the Soil Association, which certifies most British organic produce. Mainstream as it has become, organic farming still struggles with the fact that in the way we talk about it, we treat it as the deviation. But there's no semantic reason for this; we could turn it round and call organic farmers 'farmers' and the rest 'chemical farmers'.

Melchett took me for a walk. We left his house, two former labourers' cottages knocked together, clad in lavender and wisteria. A Norfolk Grey hen pecked at the wisteria flowers.

---

* A jury subsequently found that Melchett and his fellow activists had a 'lawful excuse' to attack the crop.

We passed through an orchard where the grass was up to our knees and the cow parsley grew almost as high as the trees. The apple trees were old Norfolk varieties, Sandringham Royal, Norfolk Beefing, their fruit seldom sold in supermarkets. Further on an old wood was being extended for wildlife: new oaks, beech, ash, holly and blackthorn. In a place where the ground was littered with crack willow catkins Melchett bade me not to linger. The blue crates spread out among the trees were full of bees. Elsewhere a wild-looking stretch of scrub and grass marked the place where the former owners of the land, the L'Estrange family, had allowed the gathering of furze for fuel by the newly landless poor their enclosures had created. 'We still have turtle doves migrating from Africa to the farm,' Melchett said. 'What people would have called wasteland is where the turtle doves still nest.' It was all very beautiful; a carefully thought-through and managed order with a rough, sometimes unkempt surface and abundant space for wildlife. And space, too, for crops, fertilised not synthetically but through the careful rotation of plants that put nitrogen into the soil.

It was friendlier to wildlife, and, Melchett argued, to human life, than chemical farming. It was also, by his own admission, a fiddly, labour-intensive process, and, crucially, one that produced less food than chemical farming. Melchett's cereal yields were between 60 and 70 per cent of his chemical counterparts, and shop prices correspondingly higher. He said this missed the point. Not only do such simplistic cost analyses ignore the public goods that organic farming bring; they don't take into account the hidden costs of chemical farming – the devastation of bird and insect populations, the pollution of water through run-off from the fields, the unsightliness of vast, monotonous fields. These are the opposite of public goods, public banes, and still more slippery to value. But someone has to pay in the end. 'The organic system will cost more to farm, but hugely less to society,' Melchett said. 'I'm not doing anything that will make Anglian Water spend money cleaning up the water.'

The greatest public bane, Melchett maintains, is farming's contribution to climate change. All farming, including organic, contributes to this because of the methane emitted by flatulent livestock. But where organic farming brings the financially unrewarded public good of storing high amounts of carbon in the soil, chemical farming brings the financially unpenalised public bane of enormous carbon emissions during the manufacture of synthetic fertiliser.

Here we come back to David Laborde and his point about feeding the ten billion: we can grow the food, but will the poor be able to afford it? Maximum farming – getting the most food out of the soil wherever you are by whatever means possible – means different things in different places. The high cost of fertiliser means many poor farmers in places like Africa are closer to organic than chemical farmers, through necessity rather than choice. But Laborde's fundamental point was that any deviation from maximum farming, whether to farm organically, to farm for beauty, to farm to ward off climate change, to shun GM crops, to put taste before bulk or to farm for birds rather than people, had the potential to make food unaffordable for the poor.

The implications of this depend on the interpretation. One interpretation – the raise-up interpretation – is that the protection of the environment is no less vital to the well-being of the poorest than their daily bread, and that countries like Britain should follow that philosophy both for its own people's benefit and as an example to the world. The other way of looking at it, the level-down version, is that feeding the less well-off at all levels – the relatively poor of Britain, the absolutely poor of the world – takes precedence over all else, and to restrict farmers' ability to farm big, industrially, chemically, to mass produce cheap food, is elitist at home, selfish abroad.

If the policy of the EU is increasingly tending towards raise-up, Melchett believed the native tendency of the British government, embodied in the corporate mind of the Treasury, was level-down. 'The Treasury has said for years that it is in the interests of UK plc to get food from anywhere in the world where it is cheapest. That's been the consistent Treasury view, under successive governments, which is why leaving the EU would be such a disaster for farming and the environment.'

When the English government recently had the chance to carry out its own, independent CAP reform – in agriculture, there essentially is an English government, with the four parts of the United Kingdom having separate policies – it proved eager to go on subsidising the big landowners. When the new EU subsidy regime kicked in 2015, member states were given the freedom to reduce the basic payments received by the biggest farms and shift the money towards rural development – towards stewardship schemes like Wright's. All national governments had to trim subsidy payments over €150,000 (£110,000 in 2015) by at least 5 per cent, but if they wanted to cut them by more, they could.

Seven European countries used the new powers to cut subsidies to big landowners and transfer money to smaller farmers and environmental schemes. So did Wales, Northern Ireland and, rather timidly, Scotland. In England, the government did nothing. The queen's huge farming dole stayed. The piquancy of the situation was intensified by the fact that the EU Commission and its abominator, Stuart Agnew of Ukip, were on the same side: both wanted subsidies to the big farms slashed. Melchett's certainty that a post-Brexit Britain would drop barriers to cheap imported food, and the evidence that England, left to itself, would go on subsidising big farmers, isn't necessarily a contradiction. It suggests Brexit would return the country to the pre-EEC days of duty-free imports and subsidised farmers, but with many fewer small farms, and fewer obstacles to the expansion of large-scale, mechanised, chemical farming; where British farmers would be competing with the Kazakhs, the Thais and the Kenyans in the race for the lowest prices at the checkout, rather than having Kazakh, Thai or Kenyan visitors come to marvel at the beauty of the British countryside.

There is a danger of oversimplifying the wildly heterogeneous farms and farmers of Britain. I spent time with the mainly arable farmers of Norfolk but I could have visited the dairy farmers of the West Country or the hill farmers of Northumbria or smallholders with fewer than twelve acres who don't qualify for basic subsidies. Out of 107,000 English farms that were subsidised in 2015, only 2,829 – less than three per cent – got more than £100,000, and ten per cent got less than £1,000. As the millions of people who lost their jobs through commercialisation, privatisation, globalisation and technology change will tell you, a subsidy isn't necessarily a way to get richer; it can be the only thing that lets you keep on doing what you do.

Nor can you assume farmers will have straightforward attitudes about one another. The Marquess of Cholmondeley was a 'big farmer', but his neighbour Peter Melchett liked him because he went organic. James Lake, a farmer with no farm, spoke warmly of the Cokes of Holkham, with a gigantic farm, because 'they're quite down to earth – they're businessmen now'. Melchett abhorred farmers like Agnew because they were pro-GM, yet Agnew wanted more money spent on farmer-conservationists.

It's clear that leaving the EU will leave the British country-side more vulnerable. It takes Britain out of a protected political space with a fiercely contested balance of power between environmentalists and agribusiness into an open global arena where agribusiness has the muscle.

There was a telling moment in my conversation with Agnew when he began to rage against the fact that while Britain bans the growing of GM crops, it can't ban their import, because of World Trade Organisation rules. Hang on a minute, I said. Was he claiming we'd still be bound by all sorts of overseas rules and regulations even if we left the EU, just from an agency still further away?

He blustered that a sovereign Britain wouldn't have to join the WTO. But this, for a trading nation, would be unimaginable. Outside the EU, Britain will scramble to find its niche in a harsher, more extreme environment of intercontinental trade deals. The history of privatisation, the failure to regulate Britain's wretched banks and the remorseless attacks on the BBC and the NHS all indicate that Britain's government has been rewired to accommodate multinational corporate lobbying at the citizen's expense. Why should it be any different for farmers outside the Common Agricultural Policy?

It may be a product of farmers' chronic defensiveness, but it is striking how impenetrable the language of modern British agricultural policy is to the outsider. Expressions like 'farmer-conservationist' and 'green tithe' are my own. Farmers talk about 'agri-environmental schemes' and 'Pillar 2 payments'. European Commission officials are even worse. Their original name for the grand, idealistic vision of farmers working as guardians of nature, as well as growers of food? 'Multifunctionality'. It's a pity that the language can't be clearer when all European society is asking of farmers, and offering to pay them to do, is farm more kindly. In return, with luck, for kindness back. I heard a lot from the farmers I spoke to about the selfishness of the public, on and off their farms, but the best reproach was Melchett's. When I was with him, he had nothing bad to say about walkers or cyclists or litterers on his land. He was sixty-eight and walked with the help of a stick. At one point, walking through one of his bigger fields, he swooped down with some effort, picked up an old cigarette butt, put it away and walked on, without a word of reproach.

When the referendum came a few weeks later, the rural districts of Norfolk voted solidly to leave. In the county only the university town of Norwich held out for remain, an island of European feeling separated from Cambridgeshire, the next dot in the Remainer archipelago, by fifty miles of open Leaver country. Across Britain as a whole, farmers who voted chose Leave by 53 per cent to 45 per cent. The district containing Grimsby,

Cleethorpes and Immingham, meanwhile, went heavily against EU membership, by 70 to 30 per cent.

The weeks after the referendum were a jittery and unsettling time. Life went on exactly as before, except when it didn't. In Norwich, a deli selling traditional Romanian produce was fire-bombed in the small hours of the morning. No one was hurt, although people were sleeping in a flat over the shop when it happened. A local crowdfunding appeal quickly raised almost £30,000 for the damaged business. A few days later I went with my infant son to a rally for tolerance held in the market square in response to the attack. The numbers were pitifully few. I remember looking round my fellow demonstrators and thinking none of us would be much good in a street fight. I also remember it was a warm sunny evening and the town looked its usual peaceful, unambitious self, all its history of war and sectarian strife locked away in picturesque monuments of ancient stone. My anxious imagination – perhaps not without some perverse wish for it to happen, just to show the Leavers what they were tampering with – saw a reawakening of real conflict. My sober self told me I was being a fool. This was Norwich, the town Steve Coogan made a comedy byword for English blandness and bathos.

The real event wasn't to be seen outside, but felt within. I doubt I was alone among Remain voters in feeling, for the first week or two after the referendum, that sleep-reducing ball of anxiety in the pit of my stomach which signifies the perception not just that a deeply wrong event has occurred but that the very framework within which events of any kind occur has been broken. I should have recognised the feeling sooner. It was a feel-ing I perceived intellectually, but didn't experience personally, when I talked to people in the former Soviet Union about their regret for the collapse of the USSR – its economic collapse bound together with the belittlement and dissolution of its dream-landmarks. It is a feeling, I imagine, very similar to learning that the mine or factory where you and your family have worked for a generation or two is closing, or that new people who look and talk and dress differently from your people are eligible for public benefits you've been queuing for. And now we Remainers were feeling it: people like me who had remotely observed others were experiencing it for ourselves. For Leavers the merit of voting to leave the EU wasn't only in winning. It was in getting their opponents to feel like losers – to feel what they had felt, that deep unease at the shattering of their dreamscape. My bad feeling was somebody else's catharsis.

One of the strangest things about Brexit is that a vote which was supposed to resolve Britain's situation in the world for generations didn't settle any of the urgent problems facing the country. It did nothing to challenge companies and individuals jurisdiction-hopping around the world as they grab short-term gains by suppressing wages and undermining the European principle of commonly funded universal networks of public services. Nor did Brexit resolve the economic and cultural tension between three parts of the population – the native working people of Britain, immigrants from abroad, and the growing number of retired people. The fracture between native Britons and immigrants is only a shadow of the more deep-seated, unsayable stress between the younger and older parts of the population, estranged from each other, as the result of a huge increase in life expectancy, over a greatly enlarged realm of time. Each cannot help seeing the other, on occasion, as trespassers – the young seeing the old as immigrants from the past, the old seeing the young as immigrants from the future. The arena in which these tensions play out is the National Health Service.

Unfortunately for Brexiteers, who campaigned under the lie that leaving the EU would free up £350 million a week for the NHS, the winter following the Brexit vote was the winter the NHS began to break down. It happened too soon after the referendum for the vote to have caused it, but the misdirection of political energies towards the European question distracted government from warnings of the desperate state of the health service and the closely linked system of social care for the infirm elderly.

What would it look like if the NHS 'collapsed'? Not hospitals exploding, or the dead carted off in trucks. Something more subtle, but not without loss. Everyone knows what happened to the Titanic. It hit an iceberg and sank. But suppose the Titanic had never hit the ice. Suppose, instead, it had sailed peacefully on to safe harbour on the other side of the ocean. And suppose, when the passengers disembarked, it emerged that every night during the voyage, economies by the ship's owners meant one or two of them had accidentally fallen overboard and drowned. The ship didn't sink; it was not a historic, cinematic moment of disaster. But on board, nonetheless, something had gone horribly wrong.

3

Leaving Life and Remaining

Leicestershire 2017–18

In early 2018, the year of its seventieth anniversary, the 1.3 million people who worked for the National Health Service in England found themselves in a surreal situation. They were effectively working within two realities at once, expected simultaneously to inhabit an NHS universe where a radical, highly optimistic reform programme was under way, and a second universe in which the organisation was unmistakeably close to breakdown.

In universe one, the NHS was to be upturned to give most of the healthcare people needed at home or on their doorstep. Admission to the big hospitals was only to be for patients with major trauma, or suffering diseases that demanded intensive care and complex surgical or biochemical expertise. Big hospitals would become centres of research, high technology, rare skills and dramatic, life-saving interventions. Everything else would be diffused to the community. Loosely directed by the head of NHS England, Simon Stevens, money, staff and new investment were being directed towards primary care – family doctors, community nurses, souped-up local clinics, systems to help the chronically unwell live at home.

In universe two a counter-reality prevailed: the reality of winter, the reality of need, the reality of an ever-increasing number of frail, elderly people converging on the help of last resort, the emergency hospital. That winter, as the previous winter, the system of emergency medical care in England came to the brink of collapse, with untold knock-on effects for the health system as a whole. There is evidence that in at least one part of the country, the east of England, the emergency system just plain broke.

In the whole of England there are only so many hospital beds. The number fluctuates, but there were approximately 97,000 in the winter of 2017–18, one for every 550 citizens. At the best of times, most of them are full, not only with people being treated but with patients recovering from planned operations such as joint replacements or cancer surgery. As the annual winter increase in casualties began to flood A&E, hospital after hospital ran out of beds. Staff struggled to free up space by discharging patients, but an elderly person who's technically well enough to be moved from a hospital bed isn't necessarily able-bodied enough to be simply dropped off at the home they left.

The waits in A&E for a bed got longer, and as they did, so did the waits for assessment and treatment. To make matters worse, going into winter, many hospitals were chronically short of nurses. As A&E backed up, patients waiting for beds were left for hours on trolleys in corridors, and ambulances got caught up in the jam. Paramedics aren't supposed to leave until the patient they've delivered has been seen. Increasingly, places couldn't be found for patients in the A&E reception area and they had to wait in the back of ambulances, sometimes for hours at a time. Queues of ambulances formed outside hospitals, meaning anxious and sick people were left waiting longer and longer for help. In an effort to make more space available, tens of thousands of scheduled operations were cancelled.

Hospitals in Oxford, Derby, Bath, Taunton, Leicester, Torquay, Yeovil, Warwick, Portsmouth, Northampton, Truro, Nottingham, Redhill, Gillingham, Epsom, Dartford, Maidstone, Tunbridge Wells and the Isle of Wight warned they were no longer able to provide comprehensive care. The recommended safe limit for the number of beds that should be occupied by patients in any one hospital at any one time is 85 per cent. Across England as a whole over the winter, bed occupancy averaged 94 per cent. A third of all hospital trusts reported days of 100 per cent occupancy, yet no emergency department closed, meaning those hospitals had to stow crowds of sick people in corridors. Four hospitals – Walsall Manor in the West Midlands; the North Middlesex in Enfield, North London; Hillingdon, the closest emergency hospital to Heathrow Airport; and the James Paget in Great Yarmouth – declared their beds 100 per cent full on more than half the days in that winter period.

Between them, the hospitals in Worcester and neighbouring Redditch had to divert emergency patients elsewhere at least sixty-five times. At Derriford Hospital in Plymouth, staff were stretched so thin they were unable to take breaks. Memos between managers at Southmead Hospital in Bristol in early January, leaked to the local press, warned that beds were '104 per cent full': 'Patients are admitted to any available bed,' the hospital's clinical director wrote. 'Speciality patients are scattered.' At that point, with all overflow beds occupied, the hospital still had fifty-one patients to find beds for. Stocks of face masks and walking frames were running low. It later emerged that, on various days in December, 122 people at Southmead had been left on trolleys in corridors for more than twelve hours.

In January, with Manchester's three emergency hospitals close to full, one patient had to wait more than sixteen hours to be admitted. An A&E consultant at the Royal Stoke University Hospital, Dr Richard Fawcett, broadcast his frustration on Twitter. 'It breaks my heart,' he wrote, 'to see so many frail and elderly patients in the corridor for hours and hours . . . I personally apologise to the people of Stoke for the Third World conditions of the department due to overcrowding.' Patients and their families told the local newspaper, the *Sentinel*, that corridors were so crowded with trolleys it was hard to walk down them. A shortage of cubicles meant patients were seen in disabled toilets. One eighty-year-old man, an epileptic with severe dementia who had been diagnosed with pneumonia, waited on a trolley for thirty-six hours. Photos appeared across the media showing patients – one with a drip attached – sleeping on the bare floors of Pinderfields Hospital in Wakefield. A hospital spokesman claimed that patients 'may have chosen to lie down as seats were provided'.

A whistleblower told the *Health Service Journal* that ambulance delays in the east of England had led to the deaths of at least nineteen patients and serious harm to twenty-one more.

On 1 January, an eighty-one-year-old woman in Clacton, Essex, dialled 999, complaining of chest pains. The ambulance took three hours and forty-five minutes to arrive. It was too late. A few days later, a fifty-two-year-old man in Norfolk collapsed with severe chest pain and vomiting. He was taken to the Norwich and Norfolk Hospital, but had to wait in the back of the ambulance that took him there for four and a half hours before being seen by a doctor inside the building. He was told to go home and collapsed again when he got there. Two ambulances sent to get him were diverted to other calls and by the time he returned to hospital, his life couldn't be saved.

One doctor in a major A&E department in the east of England told me he'd witnessed shortcuts taken by staff under pressure. For a time, ambulance crews had been allowed to leave patients in a hospital area that wasn't technically A&E reception. One elderly patient with abdominal pain was diverted within the hospital from emergency medicine to a GP-style consultation, sent home, returned to the hospital a few hours later, and died. 'What I've seen is the relentlessness of the shifts,' the doctor said. 'The intensity. The feeling of higher and higher accountability. And then a lack of investment in staff. Asking them to do more and more and more, to cover more and more patients. There's no give and take. The staff they should be investing in get more and more demoralised. You're at risk of creating a Mid-Staffs environment where people don't really know who they're working for and start accepting risk that previously would have been deemed unacceptable. They stop reporting things because they reported them before and nothing happened. It's creating a dangerous culture.'

What should be done?

'Stop decreasing capacity. Build capacity and build staffing. The party line is always "it doesn't affect patient care." Of course it fucking does.'

'Mid-Staffs' was a reference to the notorious ethical collapse in the 2000s at a hospital in Staffordshire where, shunned and under-resourced by reckless trust managers pursuing administrative goals, once-conscientious staff drifted away from good practice and basic decency to the point where hundreds of patients died in conditions of filth, hunger and pain.

In a letter to the prime minister on 10 January, the most senior emergency consultants at sixty-eight hospitals in England and Wales warned that the NHS was 'severely and chronically underfunded'. Chris Hopson, the head of the organisation that represented the corporate interests of NHS hospital, community and ambulance trusts, said the NHS 'no longer has the capacity to deal with the demand that it is currently facing'. Even before the winter began, Simon Stevens publicly warned his government masters that the entire system, not just emergency medicine, was teetering. Without an increase in funding, he said, five million people – almost every tenth citizen of England – would find themselves on the waiting list for an operation by 2021.

Stevens's speech, at an NHS bosses' conference in Birmingham, was surprisingly blunt and political for a civil servant, the more so because he was speaking immediately after his political chief, the government health secretary. Provocatively, Stevens compared the situation to the time of the NHS's birth in 1948 – 'an economy in disarray, the end of empire, a nation negotiating its place in the world, a need for massive house building'. Sticking the knife in even deeper, he reminded the government that it had eagerly taken ownership of a Brexit referendum result partly achieved on the basis of a promise that leaving the EU would free up an extra £350 million a week for the NHS.* He said: 'Trust in democratic politics will not be strengthened if anyone now tries to argue: "You voted Brexit, partly for a better funded health service. But precisely because of Brexit, you can't have one."'

Stevens's frustration was understandable. The two clashing universes of the NHS – the ideal of reform and transformation, the reality of frightened, confused people in pain, waiting for care in ambulances and hospital corridors – were originally linked, in the sense that a system overwhelmed by the needs of an ageing population was the dread dystopia in prospect were the transformation not to take place. But there were always three concerns lurking in the transformation agenda, set out in October 2014 in an NHS England document called, with deliberate banality, the 'Five Year Forward View'.

First, what if the government didn't come up with the money to pay for the reforms and the continued running of the organisation while they were carried out? Second, what if, instead of waiting to see whether the reforms, once bedded in, were giving the NHS some room for manoeuvre, the government and local NHS managers banked gains in

---

* 'An extra £350 million a week for the NHS' translates into a 17 per cent increase in its annual budget, which would be more than the total increase it has had in the last seven years.

advance, and 'transformation' became a euphemism for 'cuts'? And third, what if the long-predicted surge in demand from elderly people came sooner, and with more intensity, than had been predicted?

In fact, all three fears were realised. The government's claim to have protected NHS funding 'in real terms' since 2010 didn't stand up to inspection much better than the fraudulent £350 million claim of the Leave campaign. Reform was being executed not under the banner of 'transformation' but of 'sustainability and transformation', and good but experimental ideas for doing things differently were burdened, even before they started, with unrealistic projections for how much money they'd save. As for the pressures of caring for the health of a population with a growing proportion of chronically unwell older citizens, the data was imprecise, but something dramatic was happening. Between 2011 and 2018, the population of England increased by about 6 per cent. Yet the number of people who were admitted to hospital in an emergency – not those who simply attended A&E, in other words, but those among the attendees who were deemed unwell enough to need a hospital bed – went up by 15 per cent. And while the over-sixty-fives made up only a quarter of emergency attendees, they made up half of those admitted.

To suggest that the balance of England's population had shifted rapidly to the point where the great success of the NHS – giving so many people long life – had put it under strain smacked to some on the left of offering government a get-out. As if the Conservatives were being given an excuse to blame the health service's difficulties on demographics, rather than admitting that they – that is, we

– needed to put more money into it. But the two proposi-
tions weren't exclusive. The needs of the growing number
of frail elderly people were one of the main reasons the
NHS had to get more money. And no transformation in
society can occur without a transformation, planned or
otherwise, properly funded or otherwise, in the organisation that provides its healthcare.

It's hard to put concepts such as 'the growing number of
frail elderly people' and 'NHS in crisis' together with a slew
of statistics and not feel a distancing effect creeping into the
text, a certain intergenerational coldness. Unintentionally
the writer, or the administrator, or the politician, is the 'us',
the one who opines and analyses; the elderly the 'them', on
whose behalf things are done. The civil servants who
produced the 2017 update to the 'Forward View' – which
quietly sounded the alarm with the terse admission that
'demands on the NHS are higher than envisaged' – presumably meant only to inform and explain when they wrote: 'It
costs three times more to look after a seventy-five-year-old
and five times more to look after an eighty-year-old than a
thirty-year-old . . . today, there are half a million more people
aged over seventy-five than there were in 2010. And there
will be two million more in ten years' time.' Still, the last
sentence strikes an uneasy note. There are shades of the rhetoric of immigrant fear, of the neurosis that a stable, long-
established society is on the verge of being swamped by
outsiders from far away, except that these 'outsiders' were
born far away in time, rather than space. Ian McEwan openly
expressed the motif in 2017 when he looked forward to a
more liberal future Britain in 2019, cleansed of '1.5 million
oldsters, mostly Brexiters, freshly in their graves'.

It's odd, and not just because McEwan, born in the same year as the NHS, isn't exactly a youngster. In Britain, thanks to the NHS and the welfare state, our predicted life expectancy leads all, typically, to profound old age, where we will quite possibly be frail, probably carrying around a bouquet of chronic ailments, in many cases in a relationship of deep dependency – being cared for, or caring for someone more frail than ourselves. And yet there exists a psychological boundary between the elderly and the not-elderly. The not-yet-elderly know they will almost certainly cross that boundary, but until it is crossed, it is possible for the young and middle-aged to regard the old as if oldness is their essential nature.

It isn't a lack of compassion; after all, for the not-elderly, the elderly are their parents and grandparents and great-grandparents. Partly it's a problem of scale. Your mother with dementia is special: the collectivity of all mothers with dementia is a hard to grasp concept. Partly it's a problem of fellow-feeling, of immense sympathy and weak identification. It's a paradox. You can't discuss the state of the NHS without referring to elderliness as a group identity, and yet to do so is imaginatively to cut elderly people off from the accumulated selfhood of their long lives, from the greater portion of their life when they were not elderly. Which is a way the not-elderly have of insulating themselves from the inevitability of their own old age and everyone else's. Which is, in turn, a form of mass denial that makes acceptance of the health service's requirement for more cash difficult.

Chronic illnesses are common among the non-elderly, of course – diabetes, asthma, depression, eating disorders – but when we're younger, we tend to think of healthcare in linear terms: either the emergency route or, less urgently, you have symptoms, go to the GP, they prescribe something or send you to the hospital for further diagnosis, and treatment follows. In fact, as any GP will tell you, most of their work consists of managing chronic conditions. The difficult stage in the later decades of life, for elderly patients and for those treating them, is when one condition can't be tackled without taking into account a whole lot of others. In medical jargon, they're known as 'multiple co-morbidities', when in a short space of time symptoms, diagnoses and treatments begin to crowd in, overlap, interact. You can no longer be identified as a sufferer of a familiar condition: 'I'm diabetic,' 'Sarah's mum's got Parkinson's.' You become a bearer of a disease combo that probably has no name. It's possibly as unique as you are. Encounters with the health system become a struggle to make sure everyone is up to speed with your multiple conditions. It's one of life's tricks. Just when it becomes essential for strangers to care about who you are, just when your personal history is at its ripest, your medical history starts to crowd it out.

In September 2017, in Lutterworth in Leicestershire, I met Wendy Warren. She was born in Kent in 1935 and moved to Leicester just after the Second World War when her father, an engineer, found work there. She did well at school and was set to go to college, but her father lost his job and she chose to help her mother by bringing a wage into the house. She became an assistant manager in a department store. On midsummer's night in 1955 a tall, broad-shouldered farmer seventeen years her senior, John Warren, took her to the stock car racing, and a year later, when Wendy was twenty-one, they got married.

John Warren rented 175 acres from the local squire in Dunton Bassett, a village in the south-west of the county. He'd been farming it in partnership with his widowed mother, a woman tough enough to steer the tenancy after her husband died of Spanish flu in 1918. She retired and moved out after her son's marriage, and for the next thirty-six years Wendy and John Warren farmed together, growing their holding to 265 acres and living rich, busy lives. They kept a dairy herd of sixty cows. They had two daughters. John Warren raced in a motorbike and sidecar pair. Wendy Warren was a magistrate. She researched local history. She ran as a Liberal in local elections, though she quit the party over its support for joining the EEC. They decided to give up the farm in 1991 and retired to another village, South Kilworth, to a house with fine views across the countryside. Every year in early spring they spent a month in Tenerife.

When John Warren died in 2000 his widow was sixty-five, and although she was on medication for an underactive thyroid and had, unusually, developed type 1 diabetes when she was sixty, she was otherwise fit, healthy and comfortably off, able to roam the county and beyond and socialise and volunteer as busily as before.

In her early seventies, she began to suffer from macular degeneration, which made driving difficult after dark. There's no street lighting in South Kilworth and the country lanes are narrow. The village post office and shop and almost all its bus services had gradually disappeared and in midwinter, after four o'clock in the evening, Warren found herself trapped at home. A family conference was held and it was decided she should move to the market town of Lutterworth. In 2011 she was installed in a neat modern bungalow in a town where everybody knew her, with shops and its own cottage hospital and her family nearby: the community ideal.

In 2014, her eyesight deteriorated to the point where she could no longer drive. Emergency hospital visits became an annual occurrence: a diabetic coma, an ear infection. In February 2015, on her regular holiday in Tenerife, she picked up a chest infection, aggravated by a previously dormant condition called farmer's lung, caused by years of exposure to mouldy hay. Her body reacted against the antibiotics prescribed by the Canary Islands doctors and her Achilles tendons began to soften and collapse. At about the same time she developed an autoimmune condition in her leg muscles, myositis. Finding it harder to see and walk, Warren began to pay for a home help to come in the mornings. Life was becoming more constrained, although she was determined to cast her vote for Leave in the Brexit referendum in June. The chest problems never fully went away and in September 2016, after the GPs had tried three different courses of antibiotics, she was admitted to Glenfield Hospital in Leicester with pneumonia. Just before she was due to be discharged she experienced agonising abdominal pain. Her colon was leaking into her bladder through a fistula. She was taken to a second hospital, Leicester General, where surgeons performed an emergency ileostomy to divert waste from the colon to an artificial opening, or stoma, in her stomach, and allow the gut to heal. She was sent to a cottage hospital in Hinckley, ten miles west of Lutterworth, to recuperate, but in November the infection flared again and she was admitted to Leicester's third and biggest hospital, home of its emergency department, the Royal Infirmary. In December she was operated on again, the ileostomy was reversed and replaced with a colostomy, and, just before Christmas, she was transferred to Lutterworth cottage hospital to recover. In January, after more than three months in five different Leicestershire hospitals and two major operations, Wendy Warren finally went home.

At first she seemed to be recovering well. With the help of her daughters she was able to go down from three care visits a day to two. Then in early March she had to be readmitted to the Royal Infirmary. Another fistula had formed. The surgeon had to perform a second ileostomy, but couldn't reverse the previous colostomy. In April, after another short stay at the cottage hospital, she was discharged, but rehabilitation was difficult, and she moved into a care home. It was supposed to be temporary but she hasn't been able to return to her own home, except for brief visits, since then. Throughout 2017 she was a regular visitor to the Infirmary's A&E department.

When I met Warren with her daughter Joanne at her house in Lutterworth in September, I was struck by how well she appeared, despite the evidence of her medical file, how alert and full of good humour and lacking in self-pity. She had bruising from the steroid-induced thinness of her skin and, as she told me, she couldn't see my face, a few feet away. She had her legs up on the sofa (on top of everything else, she has a collapsing spine) and when she moved it was with the aid of a walker. But she came across more as a wounded soldier than a stricken old lady. When I went over the recording of our interview I noticed how full and precise her stories of her life were before her complex of conditions and how, as the narrative shifted to the last couple of years, it was her daughter who took over the role of witness.

The NHS that Joanne Warren described was one where the big central hospitals were struggling with shortages of staff and beds while the transformational steps that were supposed to ease the pressure by providing better primary care had yet to kick in. In Leicester Royal Infirmary in the winter of 2016–17, nursing staff were so pressured that they left the incontinent Warren alone in a cubicle for two hours till she was lying in her own urine. She was rescued only when the ambulance driver who was supposed to take her back to the care home found her and summoned a nurse to clean her. A shortage of pharmacists meant that patients who were ready to be discharged in the morning often weren't able to leave until late at night because their medication hadn't been approved. Administrators were so desperate to free up beds that, as Wendy Warren witnessed, porters would rouse patients with dementia in the small hours to rush them off to some part of the county where a community bed had become available. Even after the Royal Infirmary got a new, bigger A&E building in April 2017, at a cost of £48 million, the Warrens found themselves waiting outside it in the back of an ambulance, in summer as well as winter.

Against this, the Warrens could see only one clearly announced local transformation in the NHS, and it didn't make sense. Amid all the rhetoric of shifting more services from the big city hospitals to the community, the plan was to close Lutterworth cottage hospital.

In many ways Leicestershire, though landlocked, is England in miniature. It contains a densely populated, dynamic, rapidly growing city, Leicester, with a young population, full of students and immigrants, reasonably prosperous but with areas of extreme deprivation. It's on the south-eastern rim of the great jug-handle of nineteenth-century industrial boom-time cities that curves round the hills of the Peak District: Liverpool, Manchester, Leeds, Sheffield, Nottingham, Leicester, Coventry, Birmingham. Fewer than half of its 350,000 citizens described themselves in the last census as 'white British'. A third are foreign-born. It has almost as many Hindus as Muslims, and the irreligious are a larger group than the believers in any one of the big religions. All three of its MPs are Labour, among them Jon Ashworth, the shadow health secretary. It voted, narrowly, to remain in the EU.

The vales and wolds surrounding the city are very different. The 670,000 people who live in rural Leicestershire take the county's population over the million mark. There's a lot of accumulated wealth in its pretty villages and grand manor houses. Five hunts – the Atherstone, the Belvoir, the Cottesmore, the Quorn and the Fernie – still go through the motions of chasing foxes within the bounds of the law. In bleaker districts of small post-industrial towns like Coalville and Loughborough, there is poverty, low wages and anomie. Demographically it's a whiter, older world; its population is growing much more slowly than Leicester's, and that growth is among the elderly. The working-age population is shrinking. The number of over-eighty-fives is forecast to grow by 187 per cent by the late 2030s. All seven of its MPs are Conservative, among them Nicky Morgan, the chair of the Treasury Select Committee. It voted, narrowly, to leave.

If there was to be a transformation in the way Leicestershire's million people were to be helped to good health, there had to be a plan, and an organisation to carry it out. One of the curious aspects of the NHS in the Stevens era, however, was that instead of there being an organisation which made a plan, the plan came first, with the intention that it would seed the spontaneous growth of dozens of new regional organisations to tailor it to local conditions and deliver it.

As everywhere in England, the way the NHS was set up in Leicestershire, town and countryside, reflected both the hospitals and surgeries it inherited in 1948 from the old, pre-NHS world, and the successive waves of reorganisation, new builds and closures it underwent afterwards. Most recently, it was shaped by three factors: the big budget increases it received under the Labour government of Tony Blair in the early 2000s, rescuing the service from eighteen years of Conservative neglect and, at the cost of some ruinous public-private mortgages, covering the land with shiny new hospitals; the steady increase in the role of profit-making firms as NHS subcontractors, which both New Labour and the Conservatives encouraged; and the inept restructuring carried out under David Cameron in the early 2010s, sometimes called the Lansley reforms after their patron, the erstwhile Conservative health secretary Andrew Lansley.

The Lansley reforms left seven local organisations responsible for healthcare in Leicestershire. Five were part of the NHS and two weren't. There were three consortia of GPs called Clinical Commissioning Groups, or CCGs – one each for the east and west of the county and one for the city of Leicester. There was the acute trust, the University Hospitals of Leicester Trust, which ran the A&E at the Royal Infirmary (England's biggest emergency department), carried out high-end medical research and treated an array of grave illnesses. There was the community trust, the Leicestershire Partnership Trust, which treated mental illness, ran cottage hospitals like the one in Lutterworth, organised health visitors and district nurses and operated the primary care system in the county's three prisons. Two local authorities, the county council and the city council, were responsible for public health, as well as being obliged by law to look after children in difficulty and to be the carer of last resort for adults.

Post-Lansley, hundreds of these organisations – more than two hundred CCGs, and 135 acute trusts – were patch-worked across England. Stevens's NHS England laid another map on top of the old one. The country was divided into forty-four areas, each covering between three hundred thousand and three million people. Each area had to come up with a scheme for transformation. They weren't told what to do. They were given a broad menu of options and desirable outcomes and promises of packages of money if they did this or that thing. The 'they' in each of these areas was whatever set of GP consortia, hospitals and councils existed inside them. The fragmented bits of the NHS, in other words, were expected to reorganise themselves and create a radical plan for change without an explicit template being provided from above, without new legal responsibilities or powers or budgets or staff.

It was bold and risky, potentially fruitful and potentially chaotic. Politicians and health administrators in some areas, like Greater Manchester, seized the chance for a radical integration of acute and primary care, with a new set of public bodies to control a joint budget. Elsewhere, as in Leicestershire, change was more hesitant and secretive.*

The fuzziness of the process is exemplified in the acronym that was originally attached to it, STP. Normally when you introduce an acronym you spell it out. I can't with this one. The T definitely stands for 'Transformation'. The S, added at the insistence of the Treasury, stands for 'Sustainability' – a reminder that the programme is supposed to slow cost increases. But when it comes to the P, there's ambiguity. Sometimes it stands for 'Partnership', the coming together of GPs and hospitals and councils to create a single local healthcare leadership. Sometimes it stands for 'Plan'.

STP, in other words, is both chicken and egg. Leicestershire seems to have settled on the egg, the plan. Which raised the question – at least with me, when I tried to ask about it – where's the chicken? Whose plan is it? When I talked to people in Leicestershire who follow healthcare, they used two expressions: 'the footprint' to describe the area the plan covers, and 'the system' to describe the administrative machinery that produced it. Conceptually, in Leicestershire, there was a body called the 'system leadership team' – you could see public minutes of its meetings – but to the world at large this creature was shy, legally ill-defined and mute, in the sense that it lacked the equipment to respond to questions.

According to NHS England, the master of Leicestershire's STP was a career NHS administrator called Toby Sanders,

---

* Most of the new areas don't match up to single counties. The Leicestershire area includes the rural county, the city of Leicester and the tiny adjacent county of Rutland. Local healthcare insiders call it 'LLR' but, with apologies to Rutland, I'll refer to it as 'Leicestershire' to minimise acronyms.

who was also managing director of West Leicestershire CCG. But when I approached Sanders in the August of 2017, I got nowhere: initially a flat refusal, through an intermediary, to have anyone talk to me about anything to do with Leicestershire NHS, then months of vague, unrealised undertakings. It turned out that although each of the five CCGs and hospital trusts in Leicestershire had its own team of media wranglers, none of them deemed it their job to handle questions or arrange interviews about the STP. Whichever of the five I spoke to seemed unable to respond without having a meeting with all the others – and then wouldn't say anything. (Much later I heard from an insider that the predominant mood in those meetings, when the issue came up of whether it was appropriate for the NHS in Leicestershire to answer questions from a journalist about its work, was: 'What's in it for us?')

I went to a public meeting held by the University Hospitals of Leicester NHS Trust. The chief executive, John Adler, and the chairman, Karamjit Singh, held forth confidently and pleasantly about the successes and difficulties of their hospitals, without once mentioning the radical plan that was supposed to change everything – the STP. When members of the public asked questions, each one asked about the STP. Adler and Singh seemed surprised, looked at each other, and murmured that really Sanders needed to get out and spread his message.

As the months went by, I began to wonder whether Toby Sanders existed. I'd never met him or spoken to him, there was no video of him on the internet, and his Twitter feed wasn't unequivocally personal. But nobody else in Leicestershire's NHS management was ready to take up my offer of listening while they explained the virtues of the STP to me. Doctors and nurses were off-limits too. This was made clear to me when at one point, knowing better services for stroke patients recovering at home was an element of the plan, I contacted the Stroke Association, a national charity, which put me in touch with a therapist working for Leicestershire's Stroke Early Supported Discharge service. Initially she seemed happy to help, but after a few weeks of silence I called her. She said she'd checked with the University Hospitals Trust, her employer, and they'd instructed her not to talk to me. 'They told me: "Yes, we know about him,"' she said. '"He's been going around asking questions."'

Still, there was a plan. The publicly available version of Leicestershire's STP, published in 2017, reflected the two universes of reform evangelism and crisis, but because it was a single document, ways had to be found to bring the universes together, and this was awkward. That which transformed had to be shown to save money, even when there was no obvious reason it would; that which saved money had to be shown to contribute to the transformation agenda, even though, in at least one case, it blatantly contradicted it.

At the heart of the plan were two enormous amounts of money and a slogan. The amounts were £399 million – the amount by which the Leicestershire healthcare system reckoned it'd be in the red by 2020–21 if nothing changed, a fifth of its combined budget – and £350 million: the amount of capital the planners thought they'd need to invest to transform the system. The slogan was 'Home First' – the distillation of the idea that the people of England needed, for their own good, to be weaned off an over-reliance on hospitals.

'Home First' entered the culture of the Leicestershire health system in 2014 in a report by a consultant, Dr Ian Sturgess, who was called in by the University Hospitals Trust. At the time, measured by the government's national target of patients being seen within four hours of arriving at A&E, the Royal Infirmary was one of the weakest emergency hospitals in England. Sturgess saw that patients either found themselves stuck in hospital longer than necessary or were discharged in such a way that they soon bounced back. Home First, his recommended fix, focused remorselessly on unwell people spending as little time in hospital as possible: intervene early to prevent patients needing an emergency hospital admission, intervene again if a patient spends a day in hospital without something being done to speed their journey home, send them home in such a way that you minimise the risk they'll have to come back. Tag at-risk patients so that if they do return to A&E, there will be plans in place to get them home even before they arrive.

Parts of Sturgess's report found their way word for word into the Leicestershire STP two years later: '60 to 70 per cent of emergency admissions are of people with long-term conditions or frailty,' Sturgess and the STP declare, continuing in terms unintentionally redolent of the bureaucracy of criminal justice: 'These patients are known to the system.'

Home First was an admirable idea, but when it made its way from the challenges facing a single hospital into Leicestershire's broader plan, its prime aim became blurred. Was it a defensive step required by any twenty-first-century rich-world health system to prevent hospitals being overwhelmed by an ever-increasing number of frail, mainly elderly patients with multiple illnesses? Was it simply a better way to offer healthcare? Or was it a way to save money? These are three different goals, yet in the STP they were treated as if they were benefits from a single source, like a list of claimed ailments cured on a bottle of quack tonic.

Some of Leicestershire's 'transformation' elements were already in place. The area had set up a virtual 256-bed 'hospital' called Intensive Community Support, or ICS, where recovering patients were treated by nurses and therapists who drove to visit them in their own homes. Following a scheme pioneered elsewhere, most famously in Dorset, ten joint teams had been set up across the county where professionals who would previously have worked separately – district nurses, community mental health nurses, GPs and social workers – combined to give hospital dischargees a soft landing on their return home or tried to find ways to treat urgent problems without hospital care being necessary.

Much else was behind schedule, unfunded or aspirational. According to the plan, everyone across Leicestershire was supposed to be able to get access to a local doctor until 8 p.m., seven days a week, by October 2017, but this remained patchy. An essential part of the programme was to move massive numbers of outpatients – 150,000 a year, not far short of a fifth of the total – away from the big Leicester hospitals to new groups of GPs called 'federations', who would employ occasional consultants at new or re-equipped clinics and health centres in the small market towns. The STP was due to run until 2021, but this ambitious programme had hardly started. The acute hospitals were desperate to buy a new system to digitise patients' medical records, but the Department of Health wouldn't fund it.

Despite the freshness, incompleteness or uncertainty around so much of the transformation aspect of the plan, it was treated as if it had already proved itself and made it safe for Leicestershire to cut hospital beds and staff to save money. In urban Leicester, one of three acute hospitals, the General, was effectively to close. Overall acute beds would be cut by an eighth, from 1,940 to 1,697. So hopeful were Toby Sanders and his planners about the power of virtual beds and joint local teams to keep the frail unwell at home that they didn't feel the need to compensate the loss of so many big city hospital beds with an increase in rehab beds in small-town Leicestershire. Hence the axe falling on Lutterworth's cottage hospital, which was likely to be sold for development; Rutland would lose the only hospital beds it had, in Oakham.

More surprising still, given Stevens's emphasis on boosting primary care at the expense of the big hospitals, the plan called for the staff of the University Hospitals Trust to be cut by 1,500, while primary care staff would only go up by 234. In the whole of Leicestershire and Rutland, there were 568 GPs, and the STP envisaged increasing that number by a mere 1 per cent a year. Since that was the same as the area's annual population increase, it meant no real increase at all.

There were points in the plan where the measured discourse of sustainability and transformation frayed and the extreme financial pressures on the NHS glared out. One was the £250 million needed by the University Hospitals Trust to close acute services at the General and move them to the Royal Infirmary and the Glenfield. The plan envisaged that most of the money would have to come from a PFI deal, which risked adding to the deficit of the trust, which was already, like so many acute trusts, deep in the red.

The other was a severe cut of 40 per cent – £29 million – to an NHS programme called Continuing Healthcare, which funds care for severely disabled people with long-term, complex health needs, such as sufferers from Parkinson's disease or people left with spinal injuries after accidents. Across Leicestershire and Rutland, more than 1,300 people were supported in this way. For some it meant they could continue living at home. Critics pointed out that the cut might split families, with disabled people living at home being pushed away to private care facilities. Home First, in other words, as long as it wasn't too expensive.

Bart Hellyer, a former chair of the Spinal Injuries Association and a member of Rutland Healthwatch, one of the local organisations set up under the Lansley reforms to provide a voice for patients in the NHS, challenged the STP proposals at a public meeting with local NHS officials last year. When he tried to attend a similar meeting a few weeks later, he was intercepted by a security team with instructions to bar him entry, on the grounds that his wheelchair – Hellyer is paralysed from the chest down – was a safety hazard.

I visited Hellyer at his home in Rutland one day in October. The land was Anglo-Arcadian, pretty and domesticated, green and hedgerow-veined, neither hilly nor flat but gently swelling, like a sea just before the waves begin to break. It was thinly populated, with a high proportion of retirees. Wendy Warren called it 'the empty quarter'. Hellyer lived in a comfortable former lodge house in open fields near the village of Ridlington. His wife died in 2004, but he was well-off enough to pay somebody to help him do what he can't

– 'a mixture of housekeeper, carer, gardener and quite a good handywoman', he said.

Hellyer grew up in the area, went to Uppingham (a nearby private school) and studied law at Exeter. While he was there, he took part in a point to point race, his horse hit a fence, and he was shot against the ground with shattering force, breaking his spine. After treatment and therapy at Stoke Mandeville Hospital he returned to finish his degree and went on to become a pioneer of personal injury law in Britain, importing from North America the previously alien idea that damages should include the cost of rest-of-life care for people catastrophically injured in accidents. When I met him he'd retired from the law and bred racehorses from a stable in Shropshire. He'd shown extraordinary resilience in the wake of his accident, his legal work gave him prosperity and, as he readily admitted, he started life with advantages. But even if he were much wealthier than he is, he wouldn't have been able to avoid dependency on the NHS system.

It wasn't just the ambulance service, which not long ago had blue-lighted Hellyer to A&E when he fell downstairs. The NHS also provided lesser-known mobile services, obscure until you needed them, whose effectiveness required staff able to zoom across the countryside to people's homes when needed. When she was sent home from hospital, Warren came to depend on Leicestershire's small team of mobile stoma nurses. Similarly, Hellyer relied on a handful of mobile catheter crews who, in the event of a problem, stood between him and a potentially fatal condition called autonomic dysreflexia.

'If you have a blocked catheter, they have three hours to reach you or you could be dead,' he told me. 'The times I've needed it, they got to me within an hour and a half. It's a well-run service . . . but . . . if things like that are going to be needed more for people at home, what extra resources are they going to put in? If you've got all these people being treated at home, you're assuming you've got adequate transport for nurses, therapists, doctors, whatever . . . they're assumed to be able to rush around the county in the depths of winter, in the dark and cold. I've not seen one bit of paper addressing those issues. The practicalities.'

Unease had spread through the well-heeled parishes of rural Leicestershire and Rutland as the old geography of the NHS was redrawn. 'You've got big hospitals, you've got people at home, you've got the bit in the middle, the community hospitals,' Hellyer said. 'In the STP plan you're talking about taking a heck of a lot of beds out. You're taking out Lutterworth, you're taking out Oakham. The community hospital element is going to be decimated.'

When Wendy Warren was recovering at Lutterworth after her surgical odyssey through the big Leicester hospitals, it was December, and she was able to get a pass to join her family for Christmas. What will happen in similar cases after the community hospital loses its beds is murky. The 'Five Year Forward View' evoked a shift of money from big acute hospitals to local primary care, but Warren's daughter Joanne's sense that the opposite is happening wasn't surprising. While the Leicestershire STP called for £250 million to reconfigure acute hospitals in Leicester, it envisioned raising £3 million by selling off the Lutterworth hospital site, and only spending £1 million on whatever replaces it.

'Our worry is that the acute hospitals are sucking in huge amounts of money and resources,' Joanne Warren said.

'What's being done out in the rural areas with these new plans? To the huge number of older users with chronic illnesses in the rural areas it feels as if we're losing to allow that money to be sucked into the centre. Lutterworth hospital is going to be closed before they've fully proved what they're going to put in its place. That's our worry, that we're going to get a third-rate system here with fabulous super hospitals in the centre.'

Simon Hill, a campaigner against Lutterworth's closure, who praised the care his terminally ill father received at the hospital before he died in 2016, articulated the same sense of services thinning out in the countryside. 'It's not like London,' he said, 'where you can throw a stone and hit a hospital . . . There's going to be a lot of old people just dying in their homes, waiting for care.'

Joanne Warren made clear she carried no torch for the Lutterworth hospital building. 'I'd be quite happy to see it flattened and something newer and smarter put there,' she said. She was well aware of how much the NHS had improved since she was young (she's sixty). 'I remember queueing up in the old part of the Royal Infirmary. I remember this huge barn of a room where you went for a consultant's appointment. Row upon row of hard wooden seats and you could wait for hours until you were called. There is so much that's so much better. That's not what I feel we're about. If they could absolutely say: "Right, Wendy, you don't need to be in a hospital bed, we're going to send you home, because we're going to do all this at home." Are they going to provide hospital beds in people's homes?'

Warren's fragile skin made her vulnerable to pressure sores and Lutterworth hospital, like the acute hospitals, put her on an expensive pumped-air mattress. 'So where's the hospital bed that she would have needed, who's going to take her observations three or four times a day, who's going to check on all the other signs that need checking by a qualified nurse?'

In fact, hospital beds *were* being provided in people's homes in Leicestershire and Rutland. In February, six months after I'd asked the local NHS if I could meet some of the people involved in its transformation, I was finally given access to the nerve centre of Leicestershire's virtual hospital, the ICS. There wasn't much to see: a small, bare-walled, carpet-tiled room in Leicester General, with a handful of people arrayed around the edge, talking on headsets and tapping on a variety of models of well-worn computer. These were the gatekeepers of the ICS, fielding requests from other corners of the NHS to 'admit' patients to a form of hospital-like care in their own homes.

Susannah Ashton, the hospital matron, told me that while they might often order a hospital bed to be put in a patient's house, they generally deemed the conceptual 'bed' to be the patient's home. And these virtual beds might be anywhere in the thousand square miles of Leicestershire and Rutland, in the city of Leicester or out in the market towns and villages, from Sheepy Magna in the west to Frisby on the Wreake in the east.

The ICS had a staff of about 170 nurses, therapists and administrators divided into five district teams, spread out across the area, corresponding to about five 'wards' of about fifty 'beds' each. Like community hospitals, they didn't have doctors on duty; medical cover was provided by nurse practitioners, or GPs when required. Rather than a ward round, the virtual wards were subject to a board round – each team's patients and their conditions were written up each day on a whiteboard at the team base for their progress to be discussed. I saw the columns of names scrawled on the whiteboard for Leicester city: dozens of episodes of personal misfortune, predominantly falls and infections.

Rather than duty nurses in a traditional ward, with its daily cycle of meals, medication, pulse and temperature-taking, bedlinen changing and physiotherapy, the patients would see nurses and therapists more rarely, often once a day, or even less; sometimes, if a patient was deemed to have improved enough, the ICS would check in by phone. Visiting twice daily was reserved for patients whose condition was deteriorating.

Unlike the traditional district nurse or home-visit therapist, who follow a schedule of particular tasks, the ICS team, like ward nurses, were expected to react to whatever situation the patient's changing condition threw at them, even if it put their timetable out. They could order minor modifications to a patient's home – to install a key safe, for instance, if a patient had trouble answering the door. And the therapists and nurses had some training in each other's basic skills: an ICS therapist, for example, would be expected to be able to check a patient's vital signs.

On average, a patient 'stayed' in an ICS 'bed' for ten days. As Ashton described it, the prime reason for setting up the virtual hospital was to keep its predominantly elderly patients out of an actual one. The ICS was there to reassure doctors that a patient could safely do without a conventional hospital bed, and to reassure patients whose illnesses had temporarily robbed them of confidence in their ability to cope with everyday home life. 'A GP might go to see a patient at home who has an exacerbation of a chronic lung condition,' Ashton said. 'Normally the doctor would send them into hospital to get their antibiotics because they know they're quite poorly. But we can go in and support them for the next five to seven days, get them through that episode.' Compared to an actual hospital, the ICS was stripped down. It didn't operate at night, so patients who needed night care couldn't be admitted. There was no call button for a nurse; in a crisis, the patient had to fall back on the phone. Against that were the advantages of staying at home.

Ashton was enthusiastic and persuasive, bringing energy and thoughtfulness to an admirable idea. She was circumspect – a press officer from the Partnership Trust sat in on our interview – but as we talked it became clear the ICS was having to fight to realise its potential. And it wasn't hard to see why. I thought back to the post office and shop that closed in South Kilworth, one of the many reasons Wendy Warren found it tough to stay there as she got older and more infirm. It wasn't that local people didn't want those services: they did. It was that the local community couldn't offer the post office and shop a high enough reward to stay. The NHS is different. It's a national, communally funded service set up to serve a common need. If it decides it's necessary to have more services dispersed to the community – if it decides it needs to set up virtual hospitals to treat people in their own homes – it can. But it's hard to see how they won't either cost more than the services they're intended to replace, or be worse.

The numbers in Leicestershire's STP were extremely specific: a 256-bed virtual hospital would speed the consolidation of the big Leicester acute hospitals and save money by allowing the closure of sixty-five acute beds. The reality was that while the 256-bed ICS was up and running, no acute beds had closed. Had everything stayed the same, this would have left the ICS as an extra service. But things hadn't stayed the same. Even without closing any acute beds, and with the ICS operational, the system could barely cope with demand. A leaked memo from John Adler to staff in 2017 said the University Hospitals Trust was 105 beds short.

The NHS has long since ceased using the expression 'flow of patients' – staff simply refer, obsessively, to 'flow'. In Leicestershire, as everywhere else, 'flow' kept being blocked. The consequence was that those in the NHS system whose job it was to unblock the flow – by discharging patients as quickly as possible – now tried to treat the ICS not as it actually was, a useful but lightly resourced bridge to health for frail elderly people facing a spell of illness, but as the fantasy of a virtual hospital that was supposed to replace real wards in a real one. Why wouldn't they? The ICS was constantly referred to in Leicestershire's NHS documents as a hospital, and its 'beds' as if they were hospital beds.

Through the winter of 2017–18, particularly when Leicester's Royal Infirmary was so overwhelmed by emergency cases that it could no longer provide comprehensive care – a state once known as a 'black alert', now known as 'level 4' – Ashton and her team found themselves having to dig in and say 'no' when the NHS tried to discharge patients to the ICS that the ICS couldn't cope with. The tension was between one transformational organisation and another: on one side, the virtual hospital, on the other, a new organisation called the Integrated Discharge Team, which has NHS staff working alongside adult social care specialists from local councils. The team is based at the Royal Infirmary, but headed by a civil servant from Leicester City Council. 'We were finding that if people didn't know what to do with patients they would end up with us, or, at the end of the day, we were the only service still working, so they would come to us,' Ashton said. 'We weren't doing our core business because we were picking up everyone else's . . . in the last six months we've gone, "Actually, no . . . just because you're at Level 4, our taking an inappropriate patient doesn't help you in any way, shape or form because actually it blocks the flow. They'll just block a bed with us rather than with you, so in ten days you won't have another bed coming free, so there's no point." '

If saving money were the only object, there are some ways it's cheaper to have patients at home: they eat their own food, they pay for their own light and heat, they have their own sheets. But if the objective is replacing real hospital beds with equivalent care, another factor comes into play. In a traditional hospital ward, patient A is only a few yards away from patient B. In one ICS 'ward', patients A and B can be thirty miles apart. It doesn't snow inside a hospital; punctures aren't an issue when you move from bed to bed. 'The Melton Mowbray team, for example, they might have a patient on the Nottingham border and a patient who needs an IV antibiotic on the Northamptonshire border,' Ashton said. 'Well, the Northamptonshire border patient is going to take one member of staff out for pretty much the whole of the day. It's the daily game of logistics. The level of nursing staff is probably pretty similar to what you've got on an acute ward. Our challenge is the geography. The geography isn't factored into the staffing.'

Did she think the ICS would work better if they increased staff numbers to deal with the vast size of the 'hospital'?

'If you're going to really do it properly,' she said, 'yes.'

Sally Ruane, a health policy researcher at De Montfort University in Leicester, pointed out that all the indications were of a need for more general and acute hospital beds, not fewer, when numbers had already been cut to the bone. In an analysis in 2017 she wrote that the Leicestershire STP was 'premised upon a belief that expanding community-based services will permit the net closure of acute hospital beds. This is almost certainly a false premise.'

The STP's assumptions about new ways to care for people closer to home, Ruane told me, weren't evidence-based policy. It was policy-based evidence. 'You can have really good community-based care, if you've got plenty of experience, good community-based staff, and you've got a bed available in hospital,' she said. 'But the context here is they're trying to do it with limited resources.'

I asked Ruane about something else that had been bothering me. The winter scenes of sick old people waiting on trolleys and in ambulances for treatment were distressing, but they did at least draw the nation's attention to the fact there was a crisis in the NHS. Might a more diffuse kind of healthcare allow deficiencies in care for the elderly to fester unnoticed by the public at large?

'It will be much harder to know if people aren't getting the care they need,' she said. 'If an A&E is under threat, everyone in the city will know. When services are dispersed in the community, information is dispersed. It's difficult for people to know what service exists, when it's under threat, and when it needs defending.'

I asked if she'd ever met Toby Sanders. She had. 'He's young, he's slick, he'll talk you under the table. He can persuade you. He's always got an answer for everything. He's very personable.'

It wasn't until my fifth visit to Leicestershire that the system drew back the curtain a fraction and I was able to meet Sanders, in a small conference room in a modern ten-storey office block near Leicester railway station, away from hospitals and clinics, on a floor that housed only NHS administrators. The decor was quite new, but the reorganisations come fast. Over one door was a sign for a regional NHS body abolished six years ago.

Sanders sat across the table, flanked by Andrew Furlong, the University Hospitals medical director, and Azhar Farooqi, the chairman of Leicester City CCG, who was also a practising GP. It was January and the crisis in A&E departments was the lead item on the news. Furlong and Farooqi looked exhausted. Sanders was tense with energy. Tall and lean, with the physique of a dedicated cyclist (which he is), he had thick-framed glasses that made him look younger, and a slightly alarming intensity of focus. He spoke rapidly and fluently, in perfect administrative paragraphs.

'If you look at the pressures we've had over the last couple of months, and you imagine a scenario where we didn't have something like the ICS service in place, it is just a statement of fact that we would have more pressure washing back up the system,' he said. 'Could we point at [the ICS] and say we're absolutely confident it's a cheaper model? Pretty difficult to do that. Is it a model that's allowed us to expand and provide better care? Definitely.'

The University Hospitals Trust had struggled in previous years. In the winter of 2016–17, the A&E at the Royal Infirmary almost jammed solid, and when the following year the opening of the new emergency department didn't have a swift impact, the trust got a stern letter from NHS England, warning that its consistent position among the bottom ten English emergency hospitals had to end. In his leaked memo, Adler said there were weeks when the Royal Infirmary was the worst-performing emergency hospital in the country. 'Our position,' he wrote, 'disproportionately affects frail older people.'

When I met them, Sanders and Furlong reckoned there were reasons for hope at the Infirmary, in the sense that bad as things were, they hadn't got worse. Emergency admissions had levelled off; in December, attendances had fallen slightly compared to the previous year. Whether that was a result of alternatives to traditional hospitals like the ICS or measures inside the hospitals themselves was hard to say. In autumn the infirmary was 'buddied' with England's best-performing emergency hospital, Luton and Dunstable. Staff were trained to designate frail, elderly people as such from the moment they arrived in A&E, which, in the new transformational world, was equally likely to mean swift admission to a hospital bed or a rigorous questioning of the assumption that a hospital bed and subjection to a cascade of tests was in that person's best interests.

'The way we've trained doctors and clinicians is that there's almost an expectation you investigate everything,' Furlong said. 'It's about de-escalating care sometimes. Where you've got the very frail patients, it's not appropriate necessarily to do that MRI or that nth investigation – but then it's also getting people to think about the alternatives. What other sorts of care can we wrap around people? Being in hospital if you're very old and frail isn't necessarily the best place for you to be.'

Despite Sanders and Furlong's wary optimism, despite the new emergency department of glass pods and digital displays, there were still Level 4 crises at the Infirmary in the winter of 2017–18. The hospital had moved up the national league tables, but on the day I spoke to the bosses, eight of the 165 patients brought to the A&E by ambulance had to wait more than an hour to be seen. In January as a whole, later figures would show, 18 per cent of patients recognised as sick enough to need admission had to wait more than four hours for a bed. After the meeting, I discovered that a few days before, at a meeting of the system leadership team, Adler had warned that the winter emergency at the Infirmary was having a 'major detrimental effect on cancer patients'.

'We've had a lot of people come in and look at us and try and support us,' Furlong told me, 'and we are sort of standing still in a system that's deteriorating. It's very difficult to improve in a system that's going this way.'

In an organisation as corporately taciturn as the Leicestershire NHS, you look for clues in the institutional body language. I'd wanted to meet Sanders, and somebody from the primary care system, and somebody involved in running A&E – but not all at the same time. Was it intended as helpfulness, to give me what they might have assumed I wanted, the chance to bullet-point the entire Leicestershire healthcare system in sixty minutes, get on the train and leave? Or was the tension in the system such that there had to be one person from each pillar of the NHS triad

– hospital, surgery and office – listening in to make sure no one departed from the party line? Either way it was striking how ready Sanders was to adopt the role of *primus inter pares* – how ready he was to speak for the healthcare system as a whole, as if Lansley had never happened. It fitted in with a wider national trend of the STPs mutating, when they're hardly born, into a much more radical change for the NHS.

There was always something a little fake about the Leicestershire STP, not in a way that reflects badly on Leicestershire, but in the sense that it's a mixture of transformational actions the NHS and local councils were planning to carry out anyway, impractical ideas born of financial desperation, and deeds imposed on them by NHS England. The plan for two acute hospitals instead of three had been in the works for years and there were high hopes of getting money for it from the national budget under an earlier Home First–type partnership called Better Care Together: the advent of STPs actually blocked this, rather than enabling it. The ICS was set up in 2012, four years before the first draft of the STP. The STP's plans for fewer acute hospital beds, always contradicted by growing need, were likely to be supplanted by plans for more, perhaps as many as 170. And the cut in the Continuing Health Care budget was the local response to a directive from the NHS nationally.

None of this meant the transformation agenda was dead, just that it was increasingly clear the existing, fractured NHS landscape of trusts and CCGs, of hospitals and GP surgeries, would look quite different when it was carried through. The most significant achievement of the STPs wouldn't be the results of the plans, or the plans themselves, but the genesis of ad hoc integrated organisations which resulted from the requirement to produce them.

These ad hoc organisations, in turn, were the larval stage of another organisational creature. There was extreme uncertainty as to what it would look like, because none had yet appeared. As if to confuse the picture deliberately, and deter the public from taking an interest out of sheer exasperation, these mysterious bodies had already spawned multiple three-letter acronyms. NHS England envisioned that at least some STPs would evolve into something called Accountable Care Systems (ACS), which would eventually become Accountable Care Organisations (ACO). In February, dismayed by hostility among healthcare adepts to the American associations of 'accountable care', NHS England came up with a new name: Integrated Care Systems.

Since we've already had ICS standing for something else, let's stick with 'accountable care'. What is it? In the United States, it was spelled out in the Affordable Care Act, also known as Obamacare, as a way for hospitals, community practitioners and local clinics to integrate into a single system to provide complete healthcare to a set of elderly Americans receiving the form of US healthcare that most resembles Britain's NHS – the mainly taxpayer-funded, partly free at the point of delivery system for over-sixty-fives known as Medicare. Although life expectancy in the US is significantly lower than in Britain, and health spending much higher, Medicare, like the NHS, is straining to cover the medical needs of a growing population of frail elderly people. The hope was that accountable care would save money without worsening health. Instead of Medicare refunding individual doctors' practices and hospitals, and letting patients choose whom they wanted to see, primary care and acute care in an area would link up into an integrated system called an 'accountable care organisation'. Medicare would assign the organisation a lump sum, a population and a set of goals (that's the 'accountable' part, the organisation being accountable to its paymasters) and let the system work out the best way of achieving them.

To some on the left, bringing accountable care to England is a privatisation Trojan horse with the spears sticking out, and not merely because of its US antecedents. Campaigners including the late Stephen Hawking and the health policy writer Allyson Pollock have argued that the stealthy introduction of accountable care, without public debate or legislation, is illegal. In the absence of explicit legislation, they argue, there's nothing to stop accountable care organisations being or becoming commercial organisations, creating a new, controlling, for-profit layer between the government and the health service – a form of privatisation.

To Simon Stevens, the government and the King's Fund think tank, accountable care is simply a way for the NHS in some parts of England, such as Labour-controlled Manchester, to build on the STPs to break down the institutional and contractual barriers between hospitals, primary care, mental health care and social care.

It was politically inept to bring American terminology into the fraught debate over the NHS, and critics of accountable care in England were right to question the stealthy way the idea has crept towards realisation, without democratic scrutiny or legislation. For-profit health organisations are on the lookout for, and lobbying for, ways to get a foothold in the new set-up. In Nottinghamshire, for instance, the administrators behind the local STP hired the outsourcing firm Capita to advise on the shift to an accountable care system; Capita, in turn, outsourced part of the contract to the Centene Corporation, a private US health giant, much of whose income comes from acting as intermediary between the US government and recipients of publicly funded programmes like Medicare.

But there is something familiar about the concept of 'accountable care'. A single taxpayer-funded organisation working to a single integrated plan, promoting healthy life-styles, uniting doctors and hospitals and mental health care, striving to keep an entire population well in the most efficient way possible: doesn't that sound like, well, the National Health Service?

From the point of view of a conspiracy-minded American libertarian, accountable care in the United States could be portrayed as the Anglicisation of their private healthcare system – a Trojan horse for their nightmare of an American NHS. Vigilance against free market fanaticism in the UK is seldom wasted, but the accountable care idea isn't yet doomed to lead to more commercialisation of the NHS. In some ways, as sketched out, it more resembles the beginning of a return to the early, more integrated NHS. More integrated, in one respect, with the formally independent outliers of 1948, GPs, forced into a new, closer relationship with hospitals. The Americanisation of the NHS, in terms of its being twisted into a wannabe imitation of a private insurance system, was what happened from the early 1990s until recently – first under John Major with the introduction of the 'internal market', then under Tony Blair with 'patient choice', then under Lansley with the 'purchaser-provider split' and obligatory tendering of services to private firms.

After those changes, the GPs, organised into CCGs, designated 'commissioners' of healthcare, and the hospitals, designated as 'providers', were set up in such a way that each side had to meet financial targets. The trouble was they were all using the same basic sum of money from the same limited source – the government – and had no control over the price of their services. The result was chaotically misaligned incentives: it was in the hospitals' interest to see as many patients as possible, because they were paid per procedure, but in the CCGs' interest to refer as few patients as possible, because that kept their costs down. To add to the confusion, providers had to compete with private contractors for the CCGs' – that is, the NHS's – cash.*

One way of visualising each geographical area of the NHS post-Lansley was as a football team reorganised in such a way that the defenders, midfielders and forwards have to contract formally with one another for a certain number of tackles, saves, passes and goals, according to a general plan laid out by the manager, even though all the money comes from the same source: the club, and ultimately the fans. To make things more complicated, on match days, fans are encouraged to swap their tickets for another game, at another stadium, with other teams. Without the bitter memories of the ruling Conservative Party, which, having been responsible for the Lansley reforms, was now trying to bury them,

---

* This simplification greatly understates the complexity of the system, which, at the time of writing, prevails. GPs, for instance, are not just commissioners of care, but providers of it.

Stevens would probably be more forthright in proclaiming the return, area by area, of one team, one manager, one club.

In the summer of 2017, nudged by NHS England, the Leicestershire NHS system leadership quietly took the first steps towards the accountable care system. Sanders was among those who drew up the plan: accountable care, it said, wasn't 'if', but 'when'. The draft scheme was quite vague, but seemed to evoke a tearing down of the contractual barriers between the CCGs and the trusts and the creation of a single NHS organisation in the county with one plan and one budget. The councils, which hadn't been consulted, protested, but even before its STP had been finalised, Leicestershire was looking to the next acronym. The reward for those managers willing to sacrifice the time required to comprehend the full bewildering bureaucratic algebra of the new NHS may or may not be a better NHS, but is certainly a chance to define the scope of powerful new managerial jobs they alone will be qualified for.

'I'm not a big fan of the accountable care language,' Sanders told me. 'I think it has all sorts of American, privatisation connotations which are just frankly unhelpful and don't reflect what we're trying to do locally. In simple terms, it's about a more collaborative, less competitive environment. Whether you call it ACS, whether you call it a partnership . . . it doesn't really matter.'

It was unclear how accountable care would play out in the British context. Many communitarians didn't trust Stevens, who was Blair's health adviser. They saw the STPs as the realisation of a 2012 report for the World Economic Forum, aka Davos, prepared by the consultancy firm McKinsey with

Stevens, then working for the US conglomerate UnitedHealth, leading the expert input. Indeed, the report called for 'home-based, patient-driven models' of care and 'capacity reductions in higher-cost channels' – i.e. fewer people going through hospitals. And yet privatisation of the NHS as a whole can't, politically, be on the agenda: one poll suggested the public would rather see the armed forces privatised than the NHS. The direction of travel is away from patient choice and quasi-market contracts towards planning and integration. The idea that a Conservative government might allow the NHS to be more, rather than less, monolithic seems unlikely, but there is more to it. The risk to the NHS is not so much that it might be privatised outright as that it might be starved to death.

'It's not that we're getting less funding,' Sanders said. 'The funding allocations into Leicestershire will continue to increase year on year over the next five years, and that's in real terms, but the level of growth is lower than anything the NHS has known . . . if you put that alongside changes in the growth of the population, in the health of the population, it's clearly outstripping the growth in the system.' According to Farooqi, contrary to what the Leicestershire STP suggested, shifting more of the burden of healthcare from hospitals to the community wasn't going to save money, even if 'the aspiration is right'. 'I don't think the NHS is going to be able to manage on less money just because we manage people in the community,' he said.

The Conservative Party claimed to have protected the NHS from the ravages of its austerity programme since 2010 – even to have increased its budget, in real terms. It's true that compared to other areas of government spending – local government, the Home Office – the NHS got off lightly. It was also true that the NHS budget had increased by slightly more than inflation. That was the usual meaning of the expression 'in real terms'. But in the context of the NHS, the usual meaning was wrong. In real real terms, the government was cutting the NHS budget. Who said so? The government's own Office for Budget Responsibility (OBR).

Because the NHS is there for everyone in Britain, and the population of Britain is growing, the NHS needs to grow to keep pace: more staff, more facilities, more money. It's a second kind of inflation on top of the more familiar one: demographic inflation. You could measure it for the NHS by working out spending per head of population. According to the OBR, when you combined financial inflation with population growth, spending on the NHS was to be cut by 0.9 per cent per head between 2016 and 2020.

In fact, it was worse. The NHS, like other health systems around the world, faces other cost pressures. After inflation and population growth, there is the growing proportion of elderly people; the chronic conditions of modernity, particularly diabetes; and the cost of new ways to treat and diagnose people. There is one more, perhaps the biggest of all. In 1966 the US economist William Baumol noted a divergence in modern rich-world economies between industries in which people could easily be replaced by technology, such as manufacturing, and industries fundamentally reliant on people, like healthcare and education and, the subject of his study, the performing arts. His diagnosis came to be known as Baumol's cost disease.

'If car manufacturing is automated, the workers that remain share in the productivity gain with higher wages,' the economist Anita Charlesworth told me, explaining Baumol. 'If you take the viola out of a string quartet, it isn't a quartet any more. The string quartet's wages have to keep pace with the wages of the car worker, because if they don't, nobody will go and be a violinist. So all you can do is increase the price of the tickets.'

The price of the tickets, in the context of the NHS, is its budget. Unable to replace its doctors and nurses or, for the time being, cleaners and porters with machines, it's obliged to try to compete in the labour market with organisations that are doing more than they did seventy years ago with a fraction of the workforce.

To keep pace with all these pressures, until 2010, the NHS saw its budget increased, after inflation, by an average of 4 per cent a year, faster than the economy, which grew on average after 1945 by 2.6 per cent. Most of the NHS's budget increase didn't come from higher taxation. Rather, it took a bigger share of public spending as other government departments, such as defence, took less. In 2010, with austerity, all that stopped. In Britain, perilously, spending on health as a share of the economy fell. 'Pressures on the system continue to grow at 4 per cent, and funding is increasing by 1 per cent,' Charlesworth said.

In November 2017, the three big health think tanks – the Nuffield Trust, the Health Foundation and the King's Fund – blamed the funding gap for rising waiting times, routine breaches of patients' rights and rationing of services. 'The amount the government currently plans to spend,' they warned, 'is not enough to maintain standards of care and meet the rising demand for health services . . . Even if the government met all its manifesto commitments to raise

NHS funding, this would still not come close to giving the NHS the resources it needs.'

'There's no easy way out of this,' Charlesworth said. 'We have held healthcare spending down below the growth of the pressures on it in large part by holding the wages of health-care workers and trying to squeeze out efficiencies for seven years. It's pretty clear that that has run its course and we need to have a serious debate about whether we want to have a health service that's able to meet increasing needs and give access to new therapies, and if we do, we will need to pay for it.'

Baumol, who died last year aged ninety-five, worked out in 2012 that if healthcare spending in the United States continued to rise at its then rate, it would account for 60 per cent of GDP by the next century. Applying Baumol's meas-ure to Britain, the *Economist* suggested the corresponding figure would be 50 per cent. Baumol was much more posi-tive about these figures than one might imagine. He cautioned against a panic-stricken reaction of cuts and priva-tisation. Precisely because manufactured goods were becom-ing far easier and cheaper to produce, he argued, plenty of resources would be available in the economy as a whole to allow the people-heavy services such as health, education and the arts to keep on growing. By extension, robot fear – what will all the workers do when the robots come? – is misplaced: the answer is heal, nurse, teach and make art.

I see Baumol's point, but I also see, in the globalised econ-omy in general and in Britain in particular, a massive set of cultural and institutional barriers to transferring the economic gains of automation to ordinary people. The Davos report Stevens contributed to presented the general expansion of healthcare's share of GDP while other sectors of the economy automated as a looming catastrophe. The response of modern British manufacturers to efficiency gains is seldom to increase wages, because they can always find cheaper workers abroad: the reward of efficiency isn't a wage hike but the fact that you get to keep your job. Except that often you don't. The whole philosophy underlying privatisation in Britain has been that when a privatised water or energy company makes efficiency gains, it gets to keep them – generally, these days, transferring them to its overseas owners. Indeed, one of the concerns underlying the advent of accountable care in the NHS is that in the US version, when the government gives an accountable care organisation a lump sum to provide healthcare to a population, it gets to keep the difference if it does the job more cheaply. Will the same happen here? And will the money be reinvested in health, or siphoned off to managerial bonuses and private contractors? It remains unclear.

Five thousand miners lost their jobs in Coalville in Leicestershire when the pits closed. (The mines were shut in the 1980s because the coal was exhausted, rather than because of automation or foreign competition.) At about the same time, Coalville saw the closure of Palitoy, one-time maker of Action Man and *Star Wars* toys; Palitoy was bought by a US company and production moved to Asia. Recently new jobs have come to Coalville. The town is on the M1, and has become a centre for goods distribution. Amazon has built a million square foot warehouse there, which employs 600 people on mainly minimum-wage work, although there are chances for overtime. More jobs are created in parcel delivery. The Amazon system is a highly efficient way for British consumers to get the manufactured goods they want, most of them made in other countries in factories that are low wage or high tech or both: it has replaced, or wiped out, thousands of inefficient (or, to put it another way, perfectly good) retail jobs in British shops. But a Britain committed to the global economy – more so than ever, since the Brexit vote – is finding it hard to capture a share of Amazon's productivity gains to spend on the health needs of Amazon's British customers, because it's so easy for Amazon to shift them elsewhere. In 2017 it emerged that Amazon paid £7.4 million in corporation tax despite having a UK turnover of £1.46 billion. Jeff Bezos, Amazon's founder and chief executive, says he sells a billion dollars' worth of Amazon stock each year in order to fund his Blue Origin rocket firm. Bezos is engaged in a private race with another US tycoon, Elon Musk, to be the first to commercialise space travel. If Leicestershire wonders where the money for its NHS went, the answer is that some of it is on its way to Mars.

Charlesworth, who works for the Health Foundation, doesn't believe there's a political appetite for radical changes to the way the NHS is funded, even among Conservatives. Not only is it popular, it is relatively cheap, fair and, at least until very recently, effective. It's also efficient, lacking not only the casual cruelty but also the massive layers of private bureaucracy involved in the US model.

Moving to a system of workplace national health insurance, as many European countries have, would, Charlesworth points out, shift the burden of paying for the NHS onto employers and employees. The NHS system spreads payment more widely: wealthy retired people, for instance, contribute to the NHS because they pay taxes on their income if their pension is big enough.

Another idea is to separate out the health element from general taxation, so that people pay a 'health income tax' – the theory being that people would be more willing to pay more tax if they knew it was going straight to the NHS. The problem with hypothecation is that it makes health funding dependent on the ups and downs of the economy. If there were a slump and millions of people lost their jobs, NHS income would fall.

In its manifesto for the 2017 election, Labour promised to fund a hefty increase in NHS and social care spending from tax hikes on the highest-earning 5 per cent, higher taxes on private medical insurance and cutting management consultants' fees. In a globally dependent, capital-mobile Britain, would that raise enough?

Walking past Leicester Royal Infirmary one day, I caught sight of a large sports stadium a few blocks away. Ah yes, I thought, the home of Leicester City Football Club, improbable underdog Premier League champions of 2015–16. But it wasn't. It was the home ground of the Leicester Tigers rugby club (it seats 26,000). I went to a game one night at Leicester City's King Power stadium. Leicester was playing Liverpool in a low-stakes competition called the Carabao Cup, but every seat in the stadium – and every room in the city centre's hotels – was full. The strain on post-industrial Leicestershire's public services goes hand in hand with a vast, thriving leisure economy. Oakham, the town in Rutland which is set to lose the beds in its cottage hospital, has another extremely advanced, well-equipped hospital, with expert surgeons performing remarkable operations. On horses. I'm not sure what proportion of the estimated million horses in Britain are in Leicestershire and Rutland, but with such a busy hunting scene, it must be high.

Since at least the 1960s, mainstream British politics has supported, or at least failed to be greatly bothered by, the community-sapping effects of globalised consumer capitalism. People have been encouraged to believe that good public services are compatible with the frictionless movement of capital and the individualistic pursuit of play and pleasure. Suddenly, through their support for the STP process, now morphing into accountable care, the Conservatives are thrusting the sick back into the community without restoring to it the tools, the funds or indeed (how could it?) the motivation to organise their care. What the STPs offer to the 'community' is evident: responsibility without money. More subtly, it is responsibility without power. And it isn't clear that Labour's modest redistributions really get to the heart of the problem: not just a reckoning with globalisation, but a reckoning between generations.

Outside the hospital, out there in the community, people struggle with the unexpected complexities of long life and unwellness. The first time I visited Leicester, in August 2017, I went for a walk around the terraces east of the River Soar, between the railway line and Spinney Hill Park, where many Muslims live. It's an area of mosques, and few pubs, and shops that sell cumin by the pound, the area of Mohammad's Halal Fish & Chips. A woman in black drove by, her face, hands and wrists fully covered; I saw her tapping her fingers on the wheel to the beat of pounding music. It was Friday and the sun made the white garments of the men and boys gathering to go to prayer shine dazzlingly bright against the dark red brick of the houses. Watching the boys flock and jostle I felt I'd wandered into somebody's future nostalgia for an idyllic childhood. Perhaps the boy in the white dhoti who had Down's syndrome; who knows?

On one of the streets that leads steeply up towards the park I got chatting to Ahmed, who was toiling uphill with his walking frame. He had MS. He had nothing but good words for the NHS, although he noticed there were fewer nurses around these days. A man came out of his house to join the conversation. Initially he repeated the trope that Muslims have less need of public care services, that they have community, that they look after their own. Gradually he conceded that many houses in the street were regularly visited by care workers, private or state, paying their fifteen-minute visits to administer personal care to elderly people who depend on them. The street is narrow, the pavement narrow, the doors open straight onto the pavement. What made him sad was when the care workers came out of the house, ripped off their blue gloves impatiently, dropped them in the gutter and drove off to their next appointment, as if – he made the gesture of someone wiping their hands in repugnance.

Wendy Warren was an independent, civically active working woman, and in her later years she benefited from the full spectrum of twenty-first-century medicines and therapies, but there's still something timeless about her life story. She married a tenant farmer who paid rent to the lord of the manor: it's a bio that goes back millennia. Many of the generation entering old age now, those who are about as old as the NHS, had young adulthoods of determined hedonism and conscious self-destruction in the individualistic, libertarian, consumerist era that began in the 1960s. It can be shocking for them to find themselves forced into situations of communitarian dependency now.

John Knapp was the pianotron player with a Leicester band called Legay. They first gigged at the Casino ballroom on London Road in 1966, with some of their own songs and many R&B covers. They saw the Who and the Kinks. They played in, and were in the audience at, the Latin Quarter, Il Rondo, the Dungeon in Nottingham. They drank coffee in the White Cat on Duns Lane and the juke box fired them up. As mods they skirmished with leather-jacketed rockers in Nottingham. Knapp still carries a scar from where one guy stuck a screwdriver into him. The band bought the first Marshall stacks in Leicester and blew everyone's ears off. They wore make-up and got clothes from fans who worked at a theatrical costume hire shop. They wore their mod hair like crash helmets, with full fringes and luxuriant sideburns. They hid their girlfriends from their adulatory cohort of female followers. In 1967 they embraced psychedelia. They criss-crossed middle England in a van playing gigs in small towns. After they played there would be battles with local men who didn't like their effeminate clothes, or that their girlfriends fancied them. Microphone stands and cymbals were wielded as weapons. They drank and did weed, acid, coke, speed, mandrax. After their 1968 single 'No-One' failed to chart, Legay rebranded as the California Sound–inspired Gypsy, signed to United Artists, supported Led Zeppelin, did *Top of the Pops*, had their single 'Changes Coming' banned by the BBC as too political, and, in 1974, broke up. Gypsy still has a fan base, but all that remains of

Legay is memories, some scratchy recordings on Spotify and a recent book by John Knapp's brother Shaun, *High Flying Around*. It was a bestseller in Leicester.

John Knapp assumed he'd die before he was thirty. But he didn't. The band broke up before he was able to take enough drugs to finish him off, although when I met him in a pub in Leicester city centre he mused, with perverse regret, that the coke he snorted at the Speakeasy and in LA was probably of too high a quality to do the job anyway. He's sixty-nine now, but looked younger, with a dot of a beard and an elegant green linen V-neck. Rod Read, Legay's George Best lookalike vocalist, and Legay Rogers, the original drummer, died of cancer, but there wasn't much wrong with John Knapp. The unexpected, for him, was not just that he was alive, or that he wasn't in the least bit frail at sixty-nine, and didn't depend on anyone to look after him. It was that other people depended on him. He'd ended up as a paid carer at a charity-run residential centre for people with learning disabilities, many of them born with Down's syndrome.

'What does it involve?' he asked rhetorically, sipping his vodka tonic. 'Feeding them, doing personal care. They're getting old now. Dementia. Anger problems. All sorts of stuff. Don't ask me if I get something good out of it.'

Did he get something good out of it?

'Or rewarding.'

Was it rewarding?

'You now know the answer. And most people who are doing this job feel exactly the same way. It's a thankless job. It's a taxing job.'

Surely sometimes he felt quite protective towards the residents?

'You want me to be honest, don't you? No, I'm not. Because I now know these people. They're very selfish, very lazy, yeah? They are. I've worked with them now for fourteen years. The same people. You get no reward from it really.'

I looked up the centre later on the website of the Care Quality Commission, which inspects all health facilities and care homes in England. They rated it as effective, caring, responsive and well-led, but warned that it didn't have enough staff to keep residents safe.

It's minimum wage work. Knapp was expected to do a sleep-in – an eight-hour afternoon and evening shift, then an eight-hour 'sleep' on a bed in the office, then a seven-hour shift. For the entire night, when he was always on call, he got £26.

The centre was on the wane. As Knapp described it, a kind of cascade was under way: 'You know what you were talking about, the NHS doing this thing. It's the same thing, cutting down the residential and trying to get them to stay with parents . . . When anybody goes to hospital from our homes, because they've got learning difficulties, the quicker they get them out of there the better. They send them home even when they're not ready. And then they go back again.'

Knapp talked about his life as if he were re-enacting the end of the band, when he was suddenly thrust into labouring jobs. 'It's so totally demoralising because you think you've cracked it, you've had a fucking incredible life, know what I mean? I can remember always coming home at seven o'clock in the morning thinking: "All those twats going to work." When you're eighteen to twenty-two, thirty is kind of like quite a way off. And the lifestyle you're living you're thinking there's no way I'm going to get to thirty. You know. Cause we've all got addictive personalities and drugs are readily available and it's a great life so I don't want to live to thirty anyway, I don't want to be like them.' And at sixty-nine, he still doesn't want to be like them. 'I would rather die of something than end up in a home with Alzheimer's. I'd rather die than have somebody like me looking after me.'

One of the great uncertainties of the new regime is what happens to the vast realm of care that's related to health, and will regularly involve the NHS, but takes place outside the NHS's boundaries. Prominently this is about adult social care and care for children, the responsibility of local authorities, but it's also about charity-run residential centres like the one where Knapp works, about private care homes and nursing homes, and, in Leicestershire and Rutland alone, about the estimated 100,000-plus people caring for unwell or disabled family members – around one in ten of the population.

Steven Forbes, who runs Leicester city's adult social care services, pointed out to me that people with life-shortening inherited conditions like Down's were experiencing the same lifespan-lengthening marvel as everyone else, except that in their case, lifespans were doubling. 'When I started in social care someone with Down's living into their mid-thirties was exceptional,' he said. 'We now have significant numbers of people with Down's syndrome and learning disabilities who are in their sixties and seventies . . . People with Down's syndrome are particularly prone to cardiac issues, some of the neurological conditions they have as youngsters play out significantly, we've got early onset dementia. So the nature of care changes for somebody with Down's syndrome from potentially having an active life in society to caring for someone with a profound learning disability with a huge range of additional co-morbidities in their fifties and sixties and what we haven't done as a society, and a health system, is acknowledge that change. We have to acknowledge it now because it's literally standing on us. It's here. All this winter pressure is because that change we should have seen coming progressively over thirty years has now happened.'

One September afternoon I took the bus from Leicester to Coalville to visit Lee Knifton. He's a carer with an organisation called Shared Lives Plus, which matches people who need care – people who, thirty years ago, would have been institutionalised – with a lay person who has room in their home and their life to take somebody in. By mutual agreement, and with the appropriate background checks and training, the cared-for person becomes part of the carer's household, and to some extent family, with as much freedom and responsibility as they can manage. Because of the high cost of conventional residential care, there tends to be enough in the personal budget allocated by the state to the person who needs care both to support them – to pay for their food, for instance, for outings and holidays – and to recompense the carer.

I'm not sure what I expected when I got to Coalville – maybe it was the name; something grimmer? In fact the bus delivered me to a pleasant green suburb of broad streets and the spacious 1970s bungalows that have begun to look modish these days. In one of them, a sprawling, many-bedroomed place with low ceilings and fitted carpets, impeccably clean and tidy but rich with possessions, Lee Knifton lives with three men with Down's syndrome. They are clients, but they are also, in a sense, family, although Knifton has a big kindred family too: his father was one of seven brothers, all coal miners.

Knifton and two of the men he cares for – I'll call them Clem, William and Gareth, not their real names – have lived together for more than twenty years, the third moving in later. Knifton heard about Shared Lives soon after he graduated from a care course at college. It was 1997 and residential care homes were steadily shedding their clients. Like Knifton, Clem, William and Gareth were in their twenties. William and Gareth had been given up to children's homes by their parents when they were two weeks old; Clem, who as well as having Down's is autistic and has had a stroke, was looked after, on and off, in residential care until his father died, aged eighty.

The men are all in their mid-forties now. They're bound by ties that could not exist in an institution: by shared lives. Knifton is single, but not alone. 'I'm mum, dad, auntie, uncle, granny and grandad rolled into one,' he said. 'If I was having the lads now, they would only let me have Clem. I have to do everything for Clem, dress him, toilet him, feed him, give him his liquids. He can't hold a cup any more. Clem doesn't like to be touched. William and Gareth are very loving. Clem has never been able to work, whereas William and Gareth have got City and Guilds in cookery, only they can't communicate very well. William can read . . . he's good at that but not much in using initiative. Gareth, he can't read much, but he's very caring, on the ball. He'll empty the dishwasher for me.'

We were talking over tea and biscuits at the kitchen table;

the men were out. Clem was having paid recreation elsewhere. For all the comfort and security of the house, there's
a slight precarity to the situation. Knifton, a tall man with
short, bright blond hair, suffers from osteonecrosis, and,
courtesy of the NHS, has two new hips. His joints are still
causing him pain. Early last year he had a steroid injection
into his femur. It was a reminder of how interconnected the
NHS is to the wider social safety net. An elderly person can't
be discharged from hospital because austerity-wracked social
services can't place her in a care home; for that reason, an
emergency patient has to be shunted into a post-op rehabilitation bed; for that reason, a hip operation is delayed; for
that reason, a carer can no longer do his job; for that reason,
social services have another crisis.

'If I died tomorrow, they'd be all right next week,' said
Knifton. 'They've got survival mechanisms because they've
moved around so much, it's their way of coping. They are
self-centred, but that's a survival mechanism. Sometimes I get
tired and wish I could do something different but the reward
outweighs that. I don't go without, and I'm never alone. None
of us do it for money. I do love my lads. They're my family.'

Each of the men brings his own personal budget, which
Knifton must keep scrupulous accounts for (they're regularly
inspected). At the centre where Knapp works, the charity
charges residents about £700 a week. William and Gareth
have budgets of £315 a week each; Clem – 'after a long,
long fight with social services' – has £1,215 a week. 'Just to
give you an idea of how cheap we are, somebody like Clem
would be boarding on £2,000 a week in a residential home,'
Knifton said.

As social care budgets have been slashed under austerity,

local authority support for full-time carers has been pulled back. The day care centre where William and Gareth used to hang out with their peers has shut. 'They've lost their friends network,' said Knifton. 'I know society says we're clumping them all together. But people with learning disabilities like to be around other people with learning disabilities because they don't have the pressure they have when we're there. Even if I'm in the room they're always checking they're doing the right thing or not, but when their friends are there, they're always laughing and joking. We've destroyed their network of friends.

'We released people from hospitals in the 1990s and we're slowly locking people back up in nice houses in the community. There's no day care and no services for them and all they're doing is sitting at home. I can reel off ten homes now where parents are in their eighties, their children are at home with challenging behaviour, they get three days a week day care, they've been looking after them all their lives – there's going to be a crisis.'

The money councils get from central government and local taxes has fallen by 26 per cent since 2010, and the amount they can raise taxes by is tightly restricted. In the past ten years the privatised water monopolies have been allowed to increase the private tax they levy in England by 34 per cent, and keep the profits of any efficiencies they make; the government has choked council tax increases back to 16 per cent, and whenever a council shows it can scrape by after a money-saving cutback, the Treasury banks the gain and asks for more.

Like Leicestershire County Council, which is responsible for Coalville, Leicester city council has scraped by. Before Steven Forbes joined it in 2015, his department saved

millions of pounds by closing and selling off care homes for
the elderly and shutting day care centres – a significant part
of the savings coming from the fact that private and charity-
run residential homes don't pay their workers as well, or give
them such good pensions, as a local authority. Increasingly
the council's adult social care clients are aged between eighty-
five and ninety-five, often living at home, often having
outlived the remainder of their family. If they live at home,
need care and have less than £23,250 in savings and assets,
the council is legally obliged to help them out. The service is
legislated to be driven by need, not resources, and if the two
clash, Forbes's duty is to go to the mayor and tell him the
city doesn't have the cash to stay inside the law.

Already, nationwide, there are circumstantial signs of the
austerity-related funding crises in different public services
starting to join up. In Northamptonshire, where the
Conservative county council went bust, a leaked memo from
A&E over the death of a man waiting to be seen by doctors
said: 'Last night a patient died due entirely to the dangerous
overcrowding of the department.' The squalor of Liverpool's
vermin-infested prison, and the lousy management of the
recently disbanded NHS trust that provided its healthcare,
were linked to each other, but were also not unconnected to
the funding cuts each had suffered.

There are no signs of anything like this happening in
Leicestershire yet. But Forbes looks ahead anxiously to an
unaddressed funding chasm at the end of the decade. 'I think
over the last seven or eight years, with austerity, adult social
care across England has been the victim of its own success,'
said Forbes. 'We have gone out of our way to deliver those
efficiencies and savings that have been demanded by central

government. Now . . . the cliff edge is here. I can begin to feel the updraft from the edge. The measure of success in making reductions and savings – all of that's gone now.'

Forbes sits alongside senior NHS managers on the system leadership team. He and his department have bought in to Home First, transformation and integration, up to a point. They've achieved remarkable things. Putting adult social care staff into the Infirmary to work alongside NHS staff to co-ordinate the discharge of patients hasn't gone smoothly – the difference of culture between a free service and a means-tested service has been hard to bridge – but, remarkably, during the winter, only a handful of delays in getting patients home from hospital were attributable to Leicester council. Forbes has kept a reserve of social workers to go into the wards and, as he put it, 'pull those people out'.

The most striking success has been with falls. As I saw on the ICS whiteboard, a fall can quickly become a crisis for a frail elderly person. But it can also be, as it is for anyone, just something they get over. The extent to which care is still not integrated in England was brought home to me when I visited Wyggestons Hospital in Leicester, a care home and sheltered housing complex founded by a philanthropic local oligarch in the early sixteenth century. Wyggestons houses privately funded and council-funded residents. The rules are such that if a privately funded resident falls over, staff are allowed to pick them up; if a council-funded resident falls over, staff have to call an ambulance, although they're allowed to put a cushion under the victim's head.

In an effort to avoid taking people to hospital after a fall if they don't need to go, the council, funded by the NHS, runs something called the Integrated Crisis Response Service, or

ICRS. In Leicester, if someone dials 111 or 999 after an elderly person has fallen, they may well get not an ambulance but a team of council care workers to make the first assessment. Last year, of 1,500 calls for help, only 7 per cent ended up going to A&E. According to Forbes, his teams haven't made a duff call yet.

'They'll assess the individual there and then, they'll comfort them because falling is frightening, you can end up with scratches and bruises and whatever. None of that needs A&E . . . So as long as you ensure that actually nothing significant of risk has happened to them, it's mainly about the stabilisation, and if our staff think they need the paramedics' input, they bring it in.

'In the city, in this last quarter, we have actually reversed the presentation and admission of older people against the national trend. We're one of the few places that's actually stopped and slowed the increase in older people's admission to A&E. The one thing I've learned over my twenty-something years in this business is the resilience of older people and the determination of older people to remain at home, and . . . the compromises people will make in their own lifestyle to ensure their independence. We should support that. We shouldn't rush in to prevent it. Ultimately, the prize is living at home.'

Forbes, an affable Scot with a luxuriant beard who began his social work career closing wards in a 600-bed Aberdeen geriatric hospital, was convinced that the thrust of the STPs was right. After seventy years, the model of primary care based on a small private contractor – the GP practice – and the acute hospital had to change. 'We can't revert to the expectation that all older people are cared for in hospital and all people's long-term conditions are cared for in hospital. That just won't work any more. But we haven't tipped the balance of funding and investment to deal with this issue that was coming at us for thirty years.'

He was all for closer integration of primary and acute care, and a shift of funding to primary care, but the idea of integrating his service with the NHS horrified him. 'We have spent twenty years demedicalising people with learning disabilities' lives. My greatest fear is that there will be a huge and significant loss for people with learning disabilities back in a combined NHS social care entity.'

Forbes's weren't the only institutional anxieties in the age of integration. The willingness of the hospital system to integrate with the primary care system – with GPs, with community nursing – might signify the beginning, not the end, of a tussle over resources. In parts of England, hospital trusts were already taking over GP practices. One institution's 'integration' can be another institution's 'swallowing up'. What do people mean when they talk about 'keeping old people out of hospital'? Sometimes it sounds wonderfully positive, as if GPs and virtual hospitals and social workers are to be catchers in the rye for the elderly, letting them play, stopping them tumbling off the cliff of mortal illness, the cliff of an ill-judged hospital admission. Sometimes it just sounds as if the hospitals are looking for bouncers.

Hospitals – particularly university hospitals – have admirable, life-saving and often very expensive institutional goals. In any integrated county NHS set-up, they have the advantage of staff, facilities and budgets over primary care. How much will they be willing to shift the balance in the community's favour?

Shirley Barnes, a retired social worker I met in Leicester, had a twenty-one-year-old son who was born with a congenital heart condition. The children's heart unit at Glenfield operated on him and saved his life. Barnes was a stalwart of the successful campaign to save the heart unit from closure by NHS England. The intention of the closure was not to save money, but to concentrate expertise in a children's heart unit in Birmingham. The model was a new system introduced in London in 2010 to treat major trauma: after accidents the severely injured now often find themselves blue-lighted not to the closest A&E but to one further away that has more specialists and equipment. Results suggest this has saved lives. In other words, even as hospital trusts like Leicester's are being pressured from below to redistribute resources to the community, they are struggling for resources of their own to compete with NHS rivals being picked from above as high-tech regional megacentres. Hospitals are caught between extraordinary individual global dramas at the frontier of modern medicine – it was at Glenfield, in December, that surgeons saved the life of a baby born with her heart outside her body, a story that went around the world – and wards filled with frail elderly people, whose stories the world isn't interested in.

As well as a son with heart disease, Barnes had a father with dementia, Albert, who died of stomach cancer in 2012, aged ninety-one. He was a Japanese prisoner of war from 1942 to 1945: a prisoner transfer ship he was on was torpedoed and sunk, he was rescued by a Japanese trawler, and lived out the rest of the war as a prisoner in Japan. Seventy years later, demented, cancerous, deaf, half-blind with cataracts, diabetic and plagued by mini-strokes, he sneaked onto a train with £1,300 in out-of-date ten-pound notes and was found by the police, unconscious from hypothermia, curled up in a front garden in Hertfordshire. There were many such sprees in the last four years of his life, when he lived with Barnes and her family.

'It was horrendous. Absolutely horrendous,' she said. 'My dad was lovely, the life and soul of the party, absolutely hysterical, really kind, give you the shirt off his back, he was just a really, really cracking bloke, and he became this horrible – it was like invasion of the body snatchers. I was convinced that my dad was wrapped up in a pod in somebody's greenhouse 'cause it looked like my dad and it sounded like him but it weren't him.'

When Barnes took her two-week-old son to the Glenfield, a surgeon with hands like paving slabs opened up his tiny chest, went to work on his walnut-sized heart and mended it. When she went to hospital with her ninety-year-old father, they did all they could, medically; but then they sent him home, where she could never find the help she needed. The council social work department, her employer, wouldn't help, because her father didn't fit into any of their categories. In her diary she described a battle with a doctor who was reluctant to arrange a referral to get a definitive dementia diagnosis because her father had shown an occupational therapist he could climb a few stairs and make a cup of tea. 'I tell him . . . he cannot shop, cook, clean, change his bed, manage money, his paperwork, pay bills . . . I say that I have to tell him to bathe and change his clothes . . . He hides filthy clothes under his bed, behind furniture . . . I point out that I am managing all of this, along with working full-time, a husband with MS and a son who is coming up for more open heart surgery . . . [The doctor] starts to say: "We can manage the situation when he gets home." '

When you look back at life before the NHS, at local newspaper reports of people who died because they couldn't afford a doctor, the absence of indignation is palpable – indignation, that is, at the lack of free medical care. Powerful social movements and campaigning thinkers were at work, providing that indignation, but in the crowded small-font columns of the provincial press in the first half of the twentieth century another world is visible, of middle English complacency and inertia, and a feeling that if children died it was their parents' fault.

At an inquest in Tonbridge in 1914 into the death of a six-year-old girl from diphtheria, her nineteen-year-old mother, Evelyn Lambert, was accused of neglect. She said she hadn't been able to afford a doctor, and had gone on the word of a pharmacist that her child would be all right. 'The Jury expressed sympathy with the mother of the child,' the report concludes, 'and hoped that this would be a lesson to her.' In 1923, in Hammersmith, Lily Macherson, 'a poor person, of middle age', couldn't afford a doctor. Before she died, a friend tried unsuccessfully to get a police surgeon to help. The coroner asked why the police surgeon hadn't gone; 'it was a question of expense,' the police said. In 1934, Amy Bourne of Margate, starving, sick and unable to pay a doctor while her husband was out of work, lost her mind and tried to gas her two children. In Lincoln in 1924, Maud Elizabeth-Norman, a twenty-four-year-old former domestic servant, was found guilty of the attempted murder of her newborn. 'I did it because I was homeless, out of work, and starving, and I could not bear to see the child want. She had been ailing for some time. I could not afford a doctor. I threw the child in the river . . . She did not scream, and I did not see her again.' Neither the reporter who wrote the article nor the court showed the slightest curiosity as to the father of the child, although the journalist did praise the honest citizenry of Lincolnshire: 'One could not hear the story told by the various witnesses – simple, kindly country folk – without marvelling at the kindliness and charity of the people of that county towards those who wandered hungry amongst them.' Sentencing her to twelve months, the judge said: 'I hope you will take the opportunity while you are in prison to think over your unsatisfactory past.'

I'd like to think those attitudes have gone away; that the spirit of postwar communitarianism, of solidarity, in which the NHS was founded, prevails. But I'm not sure. Clearly a libertarian attitude of everyone for themselves isn't solidarity; nor is a religious attitude of 'God provides, God punishes, God rewards.' But an assumption that if only the very richest people, whom most of us neither know nor meet, were made to stick their hands deeper in their pockets, the NHS would flourish – that doesn't sound much like solidarity either. Even 'save our hospital' activists can be ambivalent. Campaigners against the closure of Lutterworth hospital assume it is a straightforward money-saving step, and ridicule the idea of replacing it with community care; there simply aren't the funds to do it properly. But when I asked them whether they would personally be prepared to pay higher taxes to fund a better NHS, they equivocated. They began to talk about how much waste there was in the health service.

Soon after I met Wendy Warren last autumn, her heart

and kidneys failed, she returned to hospital, and was told she didn't have long to live, perhaps only a few days. The family found her a nursing home in Wigston, on the southern outskirts of Leicester, and she moved in, her palliative care there funded by the NHS.

She didn't die. She got through the winter. I went to see her towards the end of February. The part of Wigston where the nursing home is has the largest proportion of over-nineties – 2.6 per cent of the population – and the third largest proportion of over-eighties, almost one in ten, in Leicestershire. Wendy had a small, comfortable room off a long corridor in a facility that felt more domestic than institutional. She couldn't leave her bed without a hoist, but she seemed the same as before, alert, with all her wits about her. At one end of the blue blanket her bare feet stuck out, the nails elegantly painted aubergine by her granddaughter. Her hair was nicely waved on the pillow.

Joanne couldn't make it; Wendy's other daughter, Louise, was there, a social worker. We sat and chatted and talk turned to the NHS. It would be convenient to be able to say that there, in the presence of somebody who's been cared for by the NHS for as long as it has existed, and who still remembers the monthly doctor's bill before that, there was an unshakeable belief in the skill of its surgeons, the care of its doctors and nurses, and the strength of an ideal of fair mutual sacrifice by the national community. But it would be dishonest, and patronising, not to report what was said, and it was doubt, not belief. Actually rather more than doubt. It was a first for me to hear somebody say, as Louise did: 'Don't get me wrong, I'm not for the work-house. But . . .'

Building up slowly, then with increasing enthusiasm, determination and evidence of considerable prior thought, Louise Warren laid out an ideal of healthcare and welfare in general that lay somewhere between mid-Victorian England and the modern, pre-Obamacare United States: an England of private medical insurance, self-reliance, self-help, of a reckoning for feckless welfare recipients who don't understand that pay TV is a luxury, of decent poor people fallen on hard times being helped by acts of charity in the same way the *Lincolnshire Chronicle*'s 'simple, kindly country folk' helped Maud Elizabeth-Norman in 1924, an England which (despite seventy years of evidence to the contrary) simply could not afford to run a national health service from public funds.

I hadn't expected to find myself suddenly having to defend the existence of the NHS in a room in a nursing home. The Warrens hadn't complained to me about the medical care Wendy Warren received. In some cases they went out of their way to praise it. When I suggested that inherited wealth in a private insurance-based health system was more unfair than small-time gaming of benefits in a welfare state, Louise Warren invoked fate as an inevitable leveller of family riches: 'My dad used to have a saying, clogs to clogs in three generations. In other words, it's not going to last for ever.'

It would be unfair to see Louise Warren as personally hard-hearted. As she said, she's not for the workhouse. As a social worker with a non-profit organisation, she helps people claim welfare benefits. For the last two decades she's been the last line of defence – apart from the police – for women and children at risk from violence and addiction. In a recent case she had to comfort a terrified client on the phone, confronted by a violent ex-partner at home in violation of a court order, and insist to the short-handed police on another line that they find an officer to protect the woman and her children. The authorities lacked the resources or will to pursue, let alone convict, the ex-partner, and the family was forced to flee their home in Leicester for the nearest safe house, 100 miles away in Manchester. But on the foundation of the NHS, Louise has a distinctive take. 'When the welfare state was set up it was never meant to be ongoing,' she said. 'It was actually to help people get back on their feet after the war.'

She'd like Britain to be more like the United States?

'They don't have as much of a welfare entitlement mentality as we do over here,' she said.

I turned to Wendy Warren, who'd been following the discussion attentively. 'What do you think, Wendy?' I said. 'Are you a liberal Liberal or a neoliberal?'

'I'm neoliberal, I suppose,' she said. 'I'm well aware that people fall on very hard times—'

'Absolutely,' her daughter chimed in.

'—and that they need support through those times. But it's very difficult. We've lost the differentiation between the deserving poor and the undeserving poor and I think that's the place where it's difficult to draw the line.'

Sometimes since the Brexit referendum I've sensed the divergent dreams of Leavers and Remainers reducing to the same primal personal desire, the desire to live in a community that is naturally, effortlessly kind to them and their families – one where a structural benignity of laws, customs and officialdom is matched by a social benignity of shared outlook and common values.

Among Leavers floats a dream of Britain as an island purged of incomers – out with the Muslim, the Pole, the Russian oligarch and his dirty money. Remainers are haunted by a dream of sanctuary, of some other country marvellously preserving the spirit of a more generous and tolerant society, ready to make available for a select few Britons that freedom and openness of outlook Britain has lost forever. 'I'm trying to get an Irish passport.' 'I'm eligible for German citizenship.' 'I'm going to be spending more time at my house in Spain. This country's finished.'

When 'dream' refers to your representation of the world, rather than to the visions that come to you when you sleep, it's not a state you're going to wake from. The disruption to your dream comes otherwise; not only in the form of a momentous event like military defeat, imperial collapse, workplace disappearance, hyperinflation, minority emancipation or Brexit. It comes when you can't avoid awareness that your dream clashes with another's: when the Remainer with her dream of sanctuary beds more and more deeply in her new home abroad only to find that there, too, resentment of the outsider and the cosmopolitan runs deep, and she encounters local versions of the dark island dream of purification she fled. Where now in the world is a sanctuary for tolerance more reliable than the one you might get if you spoke up for the values you claim to hold in the place you already are? In a United States where 73 million Americans wanted to keep Donald Trump in the White House? In a France where a third of the electorate wanted the virulently anti-immigrant Eurosceptic Marine Le Pen as president? In a Denmark which is establishing immigrant ghettos where different laws apply?

For the Leavers and their island dream, it's harsher. They know their exclusionary dream clashes with the sanctuary-seeking dream of immigrants and refugees from other countries

– people who yearn not just for better-paid work than at home but for a refuge from corruption and extreme pro-rich policies that render basic public services in their countries weak, patchy or non-existent. The whole Leaver neurosis is based on the incompatibility of the dreams of foreign sanctuary-seekers and native island-keepers – that incomers threaten not only native culture but native community security, because (as they represent it to themselves) public services are finite, like land, and more people from outside must mean less to go round for everyone. That this is, in the purely economic sense, 'wrong', is beside the point: a dream, like love or loyalty, isn't amenable to the application of fact.

What makes the resentment of the island-keepers towards the sanctuary-seekers most poignant is that their relationship is symbiotic. The Leaver dream is as much about prosperity and comfort as about cultural purity, and for that, they need the wider world. If the Leaver dream is the purely insular one of fortress Britain, it will still need immigrants to fill the tens of thousands of vacant NHS and social care posts the ageing population relies on. If it is of a revival of Britain as workshop of the world, a great exporting nation, it will need foreign customers. If it is a continuation of cheap imported goods, that will mean acceptance of low wages and weak public services in the poor world, the very circumstances that drive sanctuary-seekers to Britain's shores. It's impossible to investigate the state of mind of Britain after Brexit only by looking inwards. Other people's dreamings must be brought into play. And when it comes to dream-representations, is there another country in Europe more preoccupied with its own dream-vision of itself than Poland?

4

Leaving Work and Remaining

Somerdale 1923–2011, Skarbimierz 2010–

How to explain Poland's swing against the European Union? How to explain the election of the Catholic fundamentalist, authoritarian, populist, Eurosceptic Law and Justice Party to rule a booming country that has benefited from more than €130 billion in EU investment in its roads, railways and schools, a country where only a few years after EU accession in 2004 hundreds of foreign factories and distribution centres opened, employing hundreds of thousands of people, a country whose citizens have taken advantage of EU freedom of movement to travel, work and study across the continent in their millions? If Britain is straining the EU by leaving, Law and Justice's Poland is straining it by staying, attacking the EU's contradictory institutional positions – its promotion of human rights, its secularism and multiculturalism, its belief in state welfare, its embrace of mobile capital – with contradictory positions of its own. The typical Briton is slightly poorer now than before the financial crash, almost a decade ago; that might not be the EU's fault, but at least there's something to find a scapegoat for. The typical Pole, by contrast, is half as rich again.

Few at the richer end of Europe would begrudge rising prosperity for the hundred million Eastern Europeans who joined the EU between 2004 and 2007, 38 million of them in Poland. Whether or not Poland's rise is an economic miracle, it's an economist's miracle, in the sense that it can, and has been, used to justify most of the mainstream non-Marxist economic currents of the past century. Free traders can claim it shows how opening up a previously closed market has expanded and enriched the European economy as a whole. Neoliberals can claim that the effects of Poland's post-communist economic shock therapy – privatisation, factory closures and mass unemployment – cleared the way for the free market to come to the rescue with foreign investment and a resurgence of local enterprise. Keynesians can point to the vast amounts of public money Western Europe has poured into Poland to validate their argument that everyone gains when the state takes the lead in refuelling an economy that has run out of gas.

None of these economic ideas accommodates the triumph of Law and Justice, just as they do not accommodate Brexit and Donald Trump. Such populist phenomena are linked by their backers' ability to insist on the centrality of money-in-your-pocket economics to their cause, while at the same time promoting the primacy of romantic ideas of national and racial sovereignty in which, by definition, ideals come before money. The rise of Law and Justice and the Brexit referendum victory only make sense if economics and culture are seen as two aspects of a single field, whose fundamental substance is the collective psyche of voters; a field in which apparently unconnected economic and cultural abstractions (GDP, a lost empire) and apparently unconnected economic and cultural particularities (how much you get paid, the history of the building where you work) have links and relative weights that economics, and globalised consumer capitalism, struggle to measure. Such is the modern transatlantic dreaming.

Sometimes globalised consumer capitalism links communities in these two radically non-conformist EU states, links them, in that strange way of globalisation, without doing anything to bring them together. I looked at one such instance. It's a migrant story, but of migrant capital rather than migrant labour, and as I looked into it I began to feel that the stewards of capital who seemed the obvious beneficiaries of what was going on had lost control of their own machine. They'd programmed it to seek only one thing – efficient production – and accordingly, when the machine set about its task, it attacked the largest obstacle to efficiency, the wants of its human components, blind to the fact its programmers depended on these same human wants to validate its construction.

All factories must close one day, but there's something particularly brutal about a factory being closed because its owners have found cheaper labour elsewhere. The five hundred workers at Cadbury's Somerdale chocolate factory in Keynsham near Bristol learned on 3 October 2007 that most of their highly paid, permanent, solidly pensioned jobs were to be moved to a new factory in Poland, not because they'd done anything wrong, or because their products weren't selling, or because the factory was unprofitable, but because their Polish replacements could do the same job for less than one fifth of the money. On the day the announcement was made, the Cadbury bosses locked the workers out and posted private security guards at the site. Apparently they feared a violent reaction, but to the shocked people of Keynsham, where the lights of Somerdale had burned for eighty years, the one-day lockout looked like an attempt to project onto a guiltless workforce an act of violence that had emerged from the company boardroom.

'They didn't know the mentality of the Somerdale workers,' Amoree Radford said. 'They would have worked to the death for the factory, but the directors didn't know that.' She'd worked there for ten years and her daughter Jade and husband Les still had jobs there when the news came. Dave Silsbury, a Unite official at the factory, worked there for thirty-four years. His father had worked there; he, his brothers, his daughter and his son-in-law had jobs there when it shut. 'Cadbury was all we knew,' he said. 'We were institutionalised.' He was one of the last workers to leave, haunting its near deserted production halls, packing up for the auctioneers before the final shutdown in March 2011. By that time, the production lines had been stopped, one by one, dismantled and shipped off. The Mini Eggs production line was trucked the thousand miles to the new factory in the village of Skarbimierz in February 2010. In March, Caramel and Freddo were moved to Cadbury's Bournville plant and Fry's Chocolate Cream went to Blois in France. In June, the Crunchie bar line and Fry's Turkish Delight were moved to Poland, followed in September by Curly Wurly, and in December by Chomp, Fudge, Picnic and Double Decker.

'We watched the last few Double Deckers go through,' said Silsbury. Someone took a photo of the final Fudge to come down the conveyor.

Anna Pasternak, who worked at the new chocolate factory in Skarbimierz, noticed the age of the equipment on the production lines. The wear on the metal caused by decades of Somerdale workers' hands was the only message the British employees sent to their Polish successors. I met Pasternak in her flat in Brzeg, the nearest sizeable town to Skarbimierz. I asked her how she felt about what had happened to the British factory. 'I never really thought about it,' she said. 'We lost so many jobs here in Brzeg . . . We didn't feel sorry that others lost theirs . . . It's somewhere else in the world. We don't physically know these people.'

Somerdale had its origins in the chocolate dynasty founded in Bristol in 1753 when Joseph Fry, an apothecary, started selling drinking chocolate from his shop. He bought out a local cocoa manufacturer and the product became popular with the tourists taking the waters at Bath. A century later, the Frys were owners of the largest chocolate factory in the world. In 1847, they started making the country's first chocolate bar, Chocolat Délicieux à Manger. Like Joseph Fry, John Cadbury had gone from selling cups of drinking chocolate to manufacturing the base product, in 1831, with the help of a steam engine, in a rented four-storey building in a back alley in Birmingham. In the early years his cocoa got a warrant from Queen Victoria but by 1861, when his sons George and Richard took over the factory, now in different premises, the business was on the brink. A new product the Cadburys had been counting on to turn things around, a drink called Iceland Moss, made of cocoa mixed with lichen, failed to find favour with the public.

The first step to commercial salvation was the purchase, with the last of George's inheritance, of a machine designed by a family of Dutch chocolatiers, the van Houtens. Up to that point chocolate makers had been held back by the properties of the cocoa bean, which produced a mixture of cocoa solids and oily cocoa butter. Because it was hard to separate them, drinking chocolate tended to be greasy, heavily cut with potato flour or sago (or lichen) to sop the butter up. The van Houten machine squeezed most of the fat out of the beans, leaving cocoa solids for a purer drinking chocolate; the surplus of cocoa butter could be used to make moulded chocolate for eating.

The second stage in Cadbury's rise to dominance was its use of advertising. The openly adulterated nature of the cocoa on sale in the mid-nineteenth century had made it possible for less scrupulous manufacturers to touch up their wares with brick dust, iron filings, even red lead. Cadburys ran a national ad campaign, backed by the medical establishment, boasting of the unprecedented purity of the firm's new product, free of adulterants. Finally they used their cocoa butter surplus to enter the emerging market for mass-produced luxury goods, producing a lavish assortment of filled chocolates called the Fancy Box, decorated with the fussy sentimentality of an aspirational Victorian parlour. From there the company grew steadily through the first great age of globalisation until, in 1910, it overtook Fry, while keeping ahead of the other Quaker confectionery giant, Rowntree. The main commercial threat was the technology and business nous of the Swiss – Henri Nestlé, Rodolphe

Lindt, Jean Tobler, Philippe Suchard and Daniel Peter, the inventor of milk chocolate. Just before the end of the First World War, Cadbury and Fry undertook a defensive merger to protect themselves against takeover by Nestlé. It turned out Fry was worth much less than Cadbury; Cadbury accordingly became the dominant partner. The merger was a takeover in all but name.

One of the reasons for Fry's relative weakness was the company's failure to replace its sprawling, ramshackle network of factories in the middle of Bristol with a new factory on a greenfield site, as the Cadburys had done, moving from central Birmingham to Bournville, and Joseph Rowntree, which shifted production from urban York to suburban Haxby Road. Once the Cadburys took charge of Fry's, they enforced change, and in 1920 a site of nearly 300 acres was bought in a meander of the River Avon, a few miles east of Bristol, outside the little town of Keynsham. In 1923, the company announced a contest to give it a 'brief, easy to pronounce, striking and unique' name. The winner was 'Somerdale'.

The moves to Bournville, Haxby Road and Somerdale weren't mere efficiency and tech upgrades. In its poster announcing the naming contest Fry's says of the site: 'there is ample room, not only for factories, wharves and sidings, but also for playing fields, bathing pools and sports grounds.' The Cadbury, Fry and Rowntree families were successful capitalist industrialists, but they were also Quakers, bound to care for the welfare of their employees. In the high Victorian age it was still possible to see a potential harmony between Quaker ideals of simplicity, temperance, pacifism and charity and the handsome profits made by Quaker companies like Barclay's and Lloyd's banks, Bryant and May matches, Swan Hunter shipbuilders and Cadbury itself. In Victorian Britain, Quaker businessmen had competitive advantages. Ron Davies, in his biography of George Stephenson (Quakers were early financiers of the railways), talks about a Quaker 'moral mafia'. In a commercial land-scape filled with fraudsters and dodgy dealers, non-Quakers liked doing business with the Friends, knowing the extraor-dinary lengths the community would go to to vet its members' entrepreneurial ventures and, if things went sour, to prevent, or make good, the consequences of bad loans and bankruptcy. As for the workforce, Robert Fitzgerald, in his account of the Rowntrees, points out that since 'business and wealth were viewed by the Quakers as a God-given trust, labour could not be treated as a mere commodity'.

In fact, some Quaker industrialists treated workers very badly, notably Bryant and May. At a time when the mass of poor Britons were malnourished, under-educated, under-paid, ill-housed and unprotected against disease, Quakerism wasn't enough to make a model employer; nor were the Quakers the only businesspeople to show more than mini-mal concern for the welfare of their workers. But for decades the Cadbury, Fry and Rowntree families seemed to achieve a particularly successful synthesis of profitable capitalism and private, paternalistic welfare. At Haxby Road, Bournville and later Somerdale, there was subsidised housing, health-care and sports facilities. George Cadbury partly disinher-ited his children to build a garden village around the choco-late factory; Joseph Rowntree built the model village of New Earswick, and was an early adopter of pensions for his work-ers. The Quaker chocolate magnates wanted their factories to be handsome as well as functional. They wanted them to be surrounded by green spaces. They cared how their works appeared to God, their workers, their peers and their neighbours. Their ideology of practical, aesthetic social justice, formed at the confluence of fundamentalist Protestantism, capitalism, socialism and the Victorian fascination with an idealised medieval England, was both contradictory and, to many contemporaries, inspiring.

Over generations, the original Quaker rigour faded away under the pressure of the prosperity that rigour had brought them. In 1860, the Quakers abandoned the requirement that Friends observe 'plainness of speech, behaviour and apparel'. Edward Fry accepted the previously unthinkable worldly honour of a knighthood. George Cadbury moved into a mansion with thirty servants. In the 1930s, when Rowntree scandalised the Cadburys and the Frys by trying to patent industrial processes – some Victorian Quakers had rejected the idea of patents altogether – it was lawyers, rather than a meeting of the Society of Friends, who settled the dispute. By the 1960s, members of the Fry and Cadbury families who had shares in the merged company were clamouring for it to be floated on the stock market so they could turn their paper assets into money. In 1962, the deed was done, and Cadbury-Fry was no longer a Quaker venture.

As much as worldly success, however, it was the success of their ideals that sped the decline of the crusading wing of Quaker capitalism. Many of the liberal and socialist ideas the Rowntrees, Cadburys and Frys campaigned for, and tried to implement on a small scale, were taken up by the unions, by the Labour movement, and eventually implemented by the state. This was good and necessary, but had its downside.

The counterpart to the great privatisation of the British economy of the past forty years is the great nationalisation of culture that occurred much earlier, when swathes of life that had been covered patchily, erratically, unfairly and archaically by religion, private employers, local custom, charities, local committees of worthies and the unreliable benevolence of the rich – education, healthcare, pensions, safety at work, women and children's rights – began to be provided universally by government. It was a triumph. But it also marked a critical stage in the depersonalisation of institutional culture. It made it easier for companies whose owners have no interest in the cultural weight of the enterprises they control – who see such ideas as history, place, community, aesthetics and paternalism as outmoded obstacles to efficiency – to act as if they operate in a space outside culture, even as their decisions radically transform it.

Post-Quaker Somerdale was a decent place to work. The residual Quaker legacy, combined with the power of the unions the Quakers had embraced, meant they were well paid, with job security, good final salary pensions and paid holidays. A short walk from the heart of the factory – three long, parallel blocks four and five storeys high made of brick and steel, with enormous windows – were the sports club, the football pitches and tennis courts. In the 1970s the factory had its own chiropodist, dentist and doctor. And these benefits came without the heavy hand of Quaker paternalism. The pay was good enough to enjoy the fruits of consumer capitalism – the foreign holidays, the gadgets and appliances, the nights out and the hobbies, not just in work, but in retirement – and if some struggled to make their overtime cover a mortgage or, later in the era, their credit card debt, they knew the state, up to a point, had their back. Their children wouldn't go uneducated, and if they fell sick, they'd be cared for.

Amoree Radford gave up a job in a bank to work at Somerdale. Andy Nicholls, who headed the Unite union branch at the factory when the closure announcement came, started work there in 1972, the year before Britain joined the EEC. He'd been working as a trainee chef, earning £20 a week, when he saw an advert for a job at Fry's for £7 a week more. 'They were pretty desperate for staff,' he told me. 'Unless you were diabolical you couldn't get turned down.' He was put on six months' probation, spending four nights a week making cream teddy bears. Afterwards he went on to the Fry's Chocolate Cream production line. The company had already been making that bar for a hundred years. 'Funnily enough it was a popular bar with miners,' Nicholls said. 'They used to dip it in their tea and the glucose would melt and it would help push the coal dust down their throats.'

He was one of the leaders of the effort to persuade the Cadbury directors to change their minds about closure. He encountered a disconnect in his fellow workers' minds between what the company was doing and their image of the firm:

> There was a family feeling about the company. One of the problems we had when we got to the closure programme was people felt so much loyalty to the company they didn't want to fight for their jobs, no, 'Cadbury is telling us they want to shut down' . . . One of our problems when campaigning was discouraging members from ever

telling the press what their wages were because they were earning anything from £20–50,000. There was a lot of overtime.

Like everyone I spoke to in the West of England, Nicholls expressed no resentment towards the Poles. 'They want a job just like I do. You can't blame the Polish worker. It's the company.'

I tried to ask the members of Cadbury's board at the time about their decision to close Somerdale. There were three executive directors – Todd Stitzer, the chief executive, Bob Stack, the chief human resources officer, and Ken Hanna, the chief financial officer – and a changing cast of nine non-executive directors. Stitzer eventually walked away with £40 million in pay, pension and cashed-in shares when he left Cadbury after the company was swallowed up by another multinational, but at the time the Somerdale decision was taken the board was coming under fierce pressure from Cadbury's big shareholders, particularly the hedge fund partner Nelson Peltz and his Qatar sovereign wealth fund investors, to deliver fatter returns on their investment. I contacted the three executive directors and eleven directors – Sir John Sunderland, Roger Carr, Rick Braddock, Ellen Marram, Guy Elliott, Rosemary Thorne, David Thompson, Sanjiv Ahuja, Wolfgang Berndt, Lord Patten and Raymond Viault. Only Berndt replied (Chris Patten's assistant told me he was in 'rural Asia' without email, then, when the deadline was extended, too ill to respond). Berndt told me he couldn't remember whether the entire board had been asked to sign off on the closure, but remembered that all the directors were informed, and wholeheartedly endorsed it, 'while everybody regretted the loss of jobs'. 'It is a reality of life,' he added, 'that painful decisions like these are sometimes necessary to keep a company viable and a responsible and well-paying employer for the people who remain.'

Nicholls, Silsbury and Radford all voted for Brexit. A few years ago Radford joined Ukip. I met her in her large, comfortable house in a street within walking distance of the former factory. She was still angry about Somerdale, about the government's failure to intervene, and as we talked about chocolate-making's lack of industrial glamour, a certain amount of bitterness towards the public in general spilled out. 'You can't compare steel and mining with making choc-olate. People didn't get the history. It didn't mean anything to them. They didn't care whether they were going to get their Crunchie from Poland.'

We spent a long time talking about Britain's post-EU future. Much of what Radford said didn't make sense to me; I couldn't see, for instance, how 'We want free trade' fitted together with 'Why should we buy Chinese steel, we've got our own?' Sparring, our voices rose. Partly I still felt raw after the referendum result. But partly my discomfort was towards the institution I was defending, because I couldn't disagree that, in this case, the EU had let the people of Keynsham down badly. 'How many billion pounds did it cost us?' Radford asked of the new factory in Skarbimierz. 'Because it's in the middle of nowhere. They had to do all the roads, all the infrastructure, and that was all paid for through our donations.'

Not all; and not billions. But a sizeable proportion

– definitely. And the full story makes the EU look even worse than Radford knew.

On 10 April 1741, the twenty-nine-year-old King Frederick II of Prussia fought his first battle, in deep snow, on a low plateau to the west of the Oder, in Silesia. It was a chastening experience; he took his senior commander's advice to run away, only for the Prussian army to beat his opponents, the Austrian army of the Hapsburgs, once he'd gone. Frederick's proxy victory in the Battle of Mollwitz, named after one of three villages around the battlefield, was decisive. Silesia would, for the next two centuries, be part of Prussia and, after unification in 1871, Germany.

In the 1930s, the Luftwaffe built an airfield on the site of the battle. During the Second World War, there was a training school for fighter pilots there. In 1939, a prisoner of war camp, Brieg-Pampitz, was built near the base. Initially it held Polish and French POWs. After August 1940, it was turned into a slave labour camp. About a thousand Jews were brought from the ghettos established by the Nazis in Będzin, Sosnowiec and Czeladź and forced to work in brutal conditions on expanding the airfield. In the early years sick and exhausted Jewish workers were sent back to the ghetto, from where many would be sent on to the death camps. After August 1944, the Jewish prisoners were dispersed – those unfit for work to Auschwitz, the rest to another labour camp – and replaced by Poles from the Gestapo's Pawiak prison in Warsaw, many of whom later died during the camp's evacuation.

After the defeat of Germany, Poland's borders were shifted westwards. In the east, territories that had been part of prewar Poland, including large cities, became part of the Soviet Union (after 1991 they became parts of Lithuania, Belarus and Ukraine). Polish Wilno became Soviet, then Lithuanian Vilnius; Polish Lwów became Soviet Lvov, then Ukrainian Lviv. As it lost territory to the USSR in the east, Poland gained from the old Prussian regions of Germany in the west. German Stettin became Polish Szczecin; German Breslau, Polish Wrocław; German Brieg, Polish Brzeg. The triangle of villages around the battlefield-turned-airfield, a mile outside Brzeg, were also given Polish names. Mollwitz was renamed Małujowice. Pampitz became Pępice. The third village, Hermsdorf, was rechristened Skarbimierz.

Although Silesia hadn't been under Polish control since the 14th century, Poland's new communist government called it part of the country's 'regained lands'. Its German Jews had been slaughtered by non-Jewish Germans; its non-Jewish Germans mostly fled, were driven out or interned. Poles seeped in to the depopulated land, the majority of them from the Kresy, the lost eastern territories, and repopulated it. They took over apartments, shops and farms, changed the toponyms, and made Silesia their own.

For much of the time that Radford, Silsbury and Nicholls worked at Somerdale, Skarbimierz was a Soviet air-force base, one of the biggest in the Warsaw Pact, where squadrons of fighter-bombers crouched in readiness for war with NATO. But communist rule collapsed, the last Soviet flying unit at the base, the 781st Fighter Aviation Regiment, departed for Smolensk on 10 June 1991, and the airfield went quiet. Somerdale's nemesis was a farmer and Polish People's Party politician called Andrzej Pulit, mayor of

Skarbimierz, who looked at the derelict airfield that dominated his tiny district and thought: 'Foreign investors'.

I met Pulit in his office, in a smart new prefab put up after a bout of flooding. He was wearing a jacket and a bright red shirt, open at the neck. He was a small man with a folksy didacticism and a strong resemblance to the late magician Paul Daniels. He sat at the head of a long table. In front of him was a copy of the daily *Rzeczpospolita* with a picture of Theresa May on the front page. It was mid-January 2017 and May had just made her speech declaring that Britain, as part of leaving the EU, couldn't stay in the single market. 'May: It's A Full Divorce with the European Union,' the headline ran.

'You kicked yourself in the arse,' he said.

I told him I was a Remainer, but I did my best to put the Leavers' case to him. He didn't buy it.

'They want to close their country. Whoever does that just loses,' he said.

We talked about Somerdale. He ruminated about capital, and Jews, and when I asked what Jews had to do with it, said: 'The question is, where's the capital which rules this world? . . . I'm just making a point about who has the capital: the Jews from the USA. Of course they're all over the world, but mainly the US. It's not that we're complaining about it. This is what we've waited for, to have this capital coming, so we don't have to go around the world searching for work. And now I think our ruling party has a bad position on foreign capital. They say foreign capital is not necessarily for us. And this, in my opinion, is bullshit.'

I asked him what he'd say to the workers of Somerdale about most of their jobs being in his village now.

'I have a son in France and he earns €4,000 a month,' Pulit said. 'When he talks about it, it comes out how people work there. They take it easy. Nobody cares about their job or pays much attention to it. As far as I can see that's the difference. Our people lived through these socialist times, they experienced the transition, but there, in France, in Great Britain, they want big social benefits without any increase in productivity.'

Was he saying British workers were overpaid and lazy?

'Exactly. Gypsies go over there from our part of the world because they can get all these nice social benefits. And now that's just what's happening in Poland, because salaries have grown.'

Many agencies were involved in bringing foreign invest-ment to Skarbimierz, but Pulit claims the credit for rallying his district to get its one asset, the abandoned airfield, into shape to attract the overseas capital that would rescue the area from the ruins of communism and the free market shock therapy that followed. Cadbury already had a factory not far away, in Bielany on the edge of Wrocław, and wanted to expand, but land there cost 190 złoty (€48) a square metre. 'Here we were basically ready to give the land away,' he said. In the end they sold it to Cadbury for 5 złoty (€1.25) a square metre and promised to fix the roads and install the necessary services. To fund this the district sold off the old Soviet barracks at below market value, borrowed money, obtained government grants set aside for dealing with the legacy of Cold War military infrastructure, and got help from layers of local government above them. In the end, by one route or another, much of the money came from the EU, and although the biggest share would have come from

Germany, as the EU's biggest net donor, the next largest would have come from Britain.

Apart from the jobs Cadbury would bring, there was a direct financial incentive for Pulit and Skarbimierz. In the Polish system, the district, or gmina, the smallest unit of local government, gets the property taxes of any business on its territory. Cadbury actually decided to build two factories in Skarbimierz, one to make chewing gum and, later, the Somerdale replacement, to make chocolate. Since they opened, Skarbimierz's cluster of villages, which only have eight thousand inhabitants between them, have benefited from 18 million złoty (€4.5 million) in property taxes.

For Cadbury, the incentives were numerous. The move would replace expensive, unionised workers with cheap workers in a country where the unions are weak. Much of the cost of the new factory would be covered by selling the Somerdale site for housing. Chocolate sales in the eastern EU, Russia and Ukraine (this was before the Ukrainian rebellions and sanctions against Russia) were growing, and Skarbimierz was in the middle of the new Europe, rather than, like Bristol, out on the far fringe of its road system. It's right next to the E40, the longest designated Euro-road, which runs west in a straight line to Calais, and east through Ukraine and Russia to Central Asia. On top of this, Poland (and the EU) offered one more highly lucrative incentive. In 2007, Skarbimierz got zoned.

The idea came out of Ireland. In the 1950s Brendan O'Regan, who established the world's first duty-free shop at Shannon Airport on Ireland's west coast, realised that improved aircraft technology posed a threat to his and the area's income. The only reason flights stopped at Shannon was to refuel before

or after crossing the Atlantic; the new generation of passen-
ger and cargo jets had a longer range, and could fly between
their North American and European hubs without stopping.
O'Regan had the idea of replacing Shannon's position as a
safe haven for global travellers with a new role as haven for
global capital. In 1959 the Irish government set up the
Shannon Free Zone in and around the airport. Within its
perimeter, local and international companies who set up
factories and exported the goods overseas would be exempt
from Irish tax and duties for twenty-five years.

Companies liked this. Shannon got businesses and jobs.
Variations of the (tax) free zone have since spread all over the
world, from the maquiladoras of Mexico to the Shenzhen
special economic zone, the incubator of China's economic
rise in the 1980s. 'Shannon has been kind of an inspiration
for Chinese leaders since then,' Tom Kelleher, a near fifty-
year veteran of Shannon Free Zone and its spin-out consul-
tancies, told me. 'The Chinese embassy in London was
constantly bringing guys to Shannon, it was a kind of
Lourdes to them. Visit Shannon and you get an indulgence.'
Among the pilgrims was Xi Jinping, now China's leader, who
paid lavish homage to Shannon on a visit in 2012. Kelleher
was one of the Shannon consultants hired to design a free
zone for Poland in the 1990s. 'I think Shenzhen had started
at that stage, and somebody said: "If you want to make
progress, a free zone is the answer." The free zone was the
way you went from communism to capitalism.'

The first 'special economic zone' in Poland opened in
Mielec, in the south-east of the country, in 1995. The city
had been devastated by the collapse of work at its main
employer, an aircraft factory dependent on Soviet and

Warsaw Pact military clients. The zone was deemed a success, and thirteen others followed, all centred on areas where the economic slump was especially deep. The idea was to create business-friendly regulatory islands, but there were big financial incentives, too. Investors, Polish or foreign, were offered the chance to pay no tax for ten years, and 50 per cent tax for the next ten.

When Poland joined the EU in 2004, the rules changed. In principle the EU bans national subsidies to businesses on the grounds that it gives those companies an unfair advantage, but it makes an exception for regions that are significantly poorer than the EU average. There are many. In Britain today, Cornwall and west Wales come into this category; the whole of Poland, apart from Warsaw and its environs, does too.* Once inside the EU, Poland's special economic zones had to abide by the organisation's caps, but they were free to carry on subsidising. It's hard to know exactly how big a subsidy from the Polish government Cadbury was counting on when it made the decision to close Somerdale, but one version of the calculation, based on an investment of €250 million, would have given Cadbury a tax break worth about a third of that.†

---

* The EU has two categories of aid-eligible regions: 'a' areas like Cornwall, West Wales, Sicily or Extremadura, where GDP per head is 75 per cent or less of the EU average, and 'c' areas, where things are tough but not so bad, and permitted subsidies for investors are lower; 27 per cent of British people live in an area depressed enough to be eligible for aid. Virtually all of Eastern Europe is an 'a' area, along with Southern Italy, most of Portugal and almost half of Greece.

† Polish government figures show that from 2005 until 2016 Cadbury and Mondelez, the company that succeeded it, were eligible for about €44 million in corporation tax write-offs, although they were only able to use about a quarter of this figure.

In other words, not only did the EU pay for much of the infrastructure that enabled Cadbury to shut down its English factory and move it to Poland; it signed off on a massive financial inducement for Cadbury to go. It's the kind of thing that could give a lumbering supranational bureaucracy a bad name – although not, you would have thought, in Poland. Yet the system is coming under attack there, too, both from the defeated and scattered political left and from the victorious Law and Justice Party. At every level, from Warsaw to the regions, from government ministers to local party bosses and political appointees, you hear versions of the same seemingly contradictory Law and Justice line: we gladly take and deserve the billions of euros we get from the EU, whose cultural values we openly and contemptuously repudiate. We gladly receive and welcome the foreign investment that brings jobs, but it's a neocolonial relationship; all we do is put parts together.

'We see borders open for capital, which is a good thing, but we also see a bad side to the foreign investment in Poland and other former Soviet Bloc countries. It wasn't investment in high-tech industry,' Maciej Badora, the president of the zone where Cadbury chose to relocate, told me. 'The philosophy has been about cheap labour. They may not see it in Western Europe, but a lot of economists are pointing out that Eastern Europe has become like the post-colonial countries. To put it bluntly, we're just a big market for them to sell their products and to use our labour.'

I met Badora in Wałbrzych, a former coalmining town whose miners lost their livelihood after the fall of communism. It had an urban landscape I became used to in Silesia outside the big cities: a mix of handsomely restored (by private and public funds) old German buildings; refurbished communist-era housing; crumbling, unkempt blocks of all eras that had been rotting for decades; and the great, windowless, spick and span, low-rise slabs of factories built by the multinationals. As I drove into town, the whiteness of the snow emphasised the soot-stained lintels and cornices and window frames of unrestored stretches of old streets, like wrinkles round the eyes and mouths of miners who'd fallen asleep without cleaning the coal dust off their faces. The new industrial areas seemed to exist in a parallel dimension, adjacent, yet detached.

Badora operated out of a smart new office building tucked in among the new factories, between their loading bays and car parks and security guard booths. He hadn't been long in the job; he was a political appointee, put in place by Law and Justice after he failed to win a parliamentary seat for the party in the election that brought them to power in 2015.

Look at Luxembourg's tax breaks, he said to me, before you complain about ours.

I asked him whether there wasn't a contradiction between Law and Justice's assertion of Poland's sovereignty, its scepticism about immigration and multiculturalism and free-flowing global capital, and its seeming determination to continue embracing foreign investment and EU aid.

'If you define traditional Conservative Catholic values as, for example, honesty, hard work and social solidarity, I don't see any contradiction between these traditional values and the global economy,' he replied. 'Globalisation becomes dangerous whenever it gets rid of values.'

Speaking of solidarity, I said, what about solidarity with the British workers who lost their jobs when their factory got moved to Poland?

'Nobody can better understand this problem of closing down factories than people from our region. In this area, especially in the coalmining areas, almost all industry was liquidated in the 1990s. And we do understand that to close such a factory, especially one so long-established, is really painful and sad for local society. But decisions to close down factories are made purely by companies, and we have no influence.

'These processes are going on all over the world, and the difference these days is that Western Europe society is noticing it more. These countries, until recently, were totally indifferent; they didn't pay attention to even more painful processes going on in Eastern Europe. The only advice they had for us back then was for us to work harder. We took it as good advice.'

Talking to Poles in Silesia I was struck by the sense of economic insecurity and past, or incipient, injustice that lay just below the surface even among the administrative class. To resentful Britons, it might seem the Poles of this region are lucky: they can stay at home, where wages are rising, the infrastructure is being transformed and jobs are plentiful, or they can get work in Western Europe, where salaries are much higher. From the point of view of their Polish counterparts, this is crass nonsense. On the one hand, Poland's population is falling and its best and brightest young people are leaking westwards; on the other, the foreign capital that has brought the country prosperity has no loyalty to Poland. From Britain to Poland today; from Poland to an even cheaper country tomorrow. Poles, too, have their immigrant neuroses. As Britain is to Poland within the EU, so Poland is to its non-EU neighbour Ukraine.

'In Poland we lack doctors, and therefore we have to employ people from Ukraine,' Badora said. 'There is a huge immigration from Ukraine to our country. This is something Western Europe doesn't know. It used to be that we only saw Ukrainian workers in eastern parts of Poland. Now, even here, there are factories where 40 or 50 per cent of the workers are from Ukraine. They study here. They rent apartments.'

Criticism of the special economic zone system, which involves Poland essentially buying jobs on the global investment market in exchange for billions of euros in foregone corporation tax, is being heard more frequently from the Polish left. 'You can think of them as industrial tax havens,' said Iwo Augustynski, a Wrocław-based economist and activist with the left-wing party Razem. 'When you look at levels of corporation tax in the EU, Poland has one of the lowest. When you look at the special economic zones, it's effectively zero.'

You might assume that, because Skarbimierz is part of the Wałbrzych zone, it must be part of the town of Wałbrzych, or at least next to it. It isn't. It's eighty miles away. Since they were set up, the original fourteen special economic zones have speckled the map of Poland with scores of sub-zones, sometimes even further from their origin. The Mielec zone, for instance, near the Ukrainian border, is offering land to investors in a sub-zone 450 miles away in Szczecin, on the Baltic, as if a local investment agency in Sunderland were trying to entice investors to open factories in Dover. Odder still, in Wrocław, the capital of Silesia, a thriving, attractive, high-employment city of IT workers and service industries, zones based in depressed towns far away have bought up development sites and designated them as aid-worthy sub-zones.

'We don't have unemployment here,' Augustynski said. 'Wages are higher than average, among the highest in Poland. But we still have some zones here, and there are plans to expand them further. We have a global bank here, Credit Suisse. There's an IBM service centre, a Hewlett Packard service centre. They are all in the city centre. And they're all in special economic zones.'

Supporters of the zone system would argue that Augustynski has his sequence wrong: Credit Suisse, IBM and Hewlett Packard moved to Wrocław many years ago, not as riders of the wave, but as part of the reason the wave began to rise. They point out that the tax exemptions for zone companies do eventually expire. They could point to the recent pushback for another Swiss bank, UBS – which didn't get the zonal designation it wanted for its new service centre in Wrocław, but moved to the city anyway – as a sign of a new maturity in the Polish economy.

In 2014, too late for Somerdale, the EU recognised its error and banned the use of national subsidies to entice multinationals to move production from one EU country to another. But the EU also extended the period the Polish zones and sub-zones will be allowed to operate until 2026. And when you look at the EU's aid map of Poland, Augustynski's case becomes clearer. The poorest parts of Poland, the areas in most desperate need of jobs, are in the east. Yet the special economic zones – even, in some cases, zones in the east of the country – are helping foreign investors set up subsidised factories in the west. One of the biggest investors in thriving western Poland, just outside Wrocław, is the Korean company LG. But the sub-zone where LG built its factories was originally set up to help get jobs in Tarnobrzeg, near Mielec, 250 miles away in the struggling south-east. The explanation, according to Augustynski, is simple: the investors, the multinational firms, are in the driving seat. 'My complaint is that the main actor, the main entity who makes the decision about where this investment is, is the investor,' Augustynski said. 'It's not the local community, local government, not even the central government, it's the investor. Mercedes was the decisive example. They said, "western Poland", and when they got some proposals they chose the one that suited them best. The Polish administration is a client. It's got nothing to do with the unemployment rate in the area or structural economic problems.'

Barbara Kaśnikowska, who was sacked as president of the Wałbrzych special economic zone after Law and Justice's 2015 election victory so the new government could give Badora her job, agreed that Augustynski had a point. Sometimes foreign investors would decide where they wanted to build a factory, then put pressure on the Polish authorities to declare that place a sub-zone for subsidy purposes. (There is no suggestion that this is what happened in Cadbury's case.) But she still had faith the system was working as it was supposed to. Foreign investors who started out with simple assembly operations were staying on after their subsidies expired; they were using Polish suppliers; those Polish firms were beginning to supply foreign investors in their home countries; Poland would become a base for research. The trouble is that the party now running the country doesn't share her confidence. In October 2017

Mateusz Morawiecki, the former banker who, as the new government's finance minister, was taken in German and American boardrooms to be a reliable, globalist, business-as-usual free marketeer, an ally on the inside, gave a startling interview in which he denounced rich Western countries for conspiring to keep Poland in a state of economic dependency. 'Having reached a peak of development themselves, the rich countries are now defending deregulation, the liberal approach, globalisation, because it suits them,' he said. The IMF itself, he claimed, had concluded that 'in countries like Poland the cost of the traditional neoliberal model exceeded the benefit.'*

The chocolate factory was built as planned in Skarbimierz, except for one detail: it no longer belonged to Cadbury. A few months before Skarbimierz began production in 2010, Cadbury was bought for £11.5 billion in a hostile takeover by Kraft Foods, a US conglomerate four times its size. During the takeover, Kraft had promised to keep production at Somerdale, but once it had the British company, it reneged and went ahead with the closure. Two years later, Kraft spun off its stagnant North American processed foods business, leaving a vast global enterprise that it hoped would grow through heavy marketing of sugary snacks to newly prosperous families in India, Latin America, Africa, east Asia and Eastern Europe – households, for instance, with family members who worked in a new factory built by a multinational. After an internal contest to find a name for the

---

* In December 2017, Morawiecki replaced Beata Szydło as Poland's prime minister.

reconfigured company, it was called Mondelez, meaning 'world delicious' in a nonce pidgin Esperanto.

From Wrocław, where I stayed, it was less than an hour's drive along the E40 to the Mondelez factories in Skarbimierz. You leave the solid grandeur of central Wrocław and the jostle of its shiny new office districts (the city was almost destroyed in 1945, when it was one of the last Nazi strongholds to fall to the Red Army) and hit the new factory and warehouse areas. Modern factory architecture, low, windowless, hangar-like, looms all around. No matter how close you get, the buildings lie: they never stand. The exit from Wrocław is marked by a sprawling Tesco, an enormous Ikea (not that there are non-enormous versions), the older Mondelez factory – still with its Cadbury sign – and by Amazon warehouses bigger than any of them. Factories on the flat horizon mark the land, but they aren't landmarks.

The two new Mondelez factories in Skarbimierz, one for gum and one for chocolate, have roofed over seven and a half acres. The chocolate factory is a giant shed, a blank oblong with a series of slightly higher blank oblongs jutting out of it. Most new factories are monochrome but the Mondelez factory is two-tone – grey and another, darker grey. It is digital-neat, as if it hadn't so much been built as computer-rendered onto the bright white snow. On either side are other industrial sheds, nodes in the global supply chain: a distribution centre for the Portuguese food company Jerónimo Martins, an air filter plant built by the Minneapolis firm Donaldson and a car-seat maker, Johnson Controls, based in Wisconsin.

There's a set of turnstiles in the fence around the factory but nobody stopped me going through. A sign promoted a kind of managerial cult called Integrated Lean 6 Sigma, designed to reduce defects on the production line. A slogan in multicoloured letters on the corner of the factory exhorted employees to WORK, HAVE FUN, AND LIVE SAFELY. I peered through the glass entrance doors. Another poster read CONNECTED THROUGH JOY. A quizzical security guard wandered towards me. I hadn't told Mondelez I was coming. I made myself scarce.

Just behind the factory, the remains of the old runway are still there. Driving along the road on the far side of the plant you start to see the characteristic shape of military aircraft shelters among the trees, barn-like structures with thick walls and heavy metal doors designed to protect Soviet aircraft from attack by NATO. I had lunch in a restaurant close to the industrial area. Judging by the decor and the prices it was aimed at the new executive class, the supplier representatives, the local managers and the head office mandarins passing through on inspection. I found out later that there's a memorial nearby to the labour camp, put up by local Polish groups in 1998. The inscription reads 'Prisoners of various nationalities worked here on the construction of the local airfield; among them were soldiers of the Polish national army, many of whom were killed.' The plaque bears the Christian cross and the Kotwica, the wartime symbol of the Polish resistance, later adopted by anti-communists. There is no Jewish star.

The block in Brzeg where the former chocolate factory worker Anna Pasternak lives, a five-storey prewar German apartment building, had just been restored and painted cream and green, the stucco swags around the bullseye windows in the loft painstakingly re-created. A small red sign in front directs patrons to an Erotic Shop down a side street. On the other side of the road, a building once the equal of Pasternak's stands derelict, sprayed with tags, its windows smashed, crumbling brickwork shedding plaster. Further along are twin fourteen-storey communist-era tower blocks, perilously conjoined by a flimsy walkway at their top corners, their recent coat of jaunty pink starting to grime up.

Pasternak's parents, who bought the flat from the state, recently handed it over to her and retired to their hometown in the east of the country. The flat has big rooms, high ceilings, yellow and lime walls, and an enormous pot plant towering over the TV. Pasternak was on her laptop when I arrived. Its cooling system was broken and she had it sat on her coffee table on a layer of empty dessert tins to stop it overheating. She's thirty-seven years old, an engineer and an improviser, and her work history is a paradigm of Silesia's recent economic frenzy. She finished high school in 2003 and began an eight-year course of studies at a series of vocational schools, learning to build, control and manage assembly lines. From the start, she worked at the same time, studying at the weekend and working all week. Her first job was at a chicken factory in Opole, the capital of the province where Brzeg and Skarbimierz lie, up the river Oder in the opposite direction from Wrocław. Every day the chicken factory bus would pick Pasternak up from Brzeg at 4.05 a.m. and wind through a string of villages, gathering workers. 'It took around one and a half hours to get to the factory, you did eight hours' work, and you were home by 3.45. We started with a live chicken, then it was cut and processed and it would come out on trays. It wasn't very skilled. The requirements were not high. You just had to have been to school, have a health certificate and be willing to work.' She got 850 złoty a month, cash in hand, about €212 at today's exchange rates. 'It lasted ten months,' she said. 'They fired me when they found out I was studying.'

Her next job was on the checkout of one of the foreign supermarkets that had rushed into Poland on accession. There she only got 800 złoty a month (€200) but she was glad of the work. 'Back then you would take any job. The unemployment round here was around 50 or 60 per cent so if you got any job you clung to it with your hands and feet.

'The supermarkets came in kind of gradually, and then, when the chewing gum factory was built, there was another factory, another, boom, boom! People were glad. Suddenly we could choose to work here, or there.'

In 2005, Toyota built a diesel engine factory in one of the Wałbrzych sub-zones fifteen miles away. Pasternak got a job on the production line. It was her first experience of working as one human component in a multinational, in a single global manufacturing, assembling and distribution system, encompassing more than 300,000 workers in fifty-three factories in twenty-eight countries. The work consisted of a single set of procedures, lasting a minute, that she'd repeat 445 times in the course of an eight-hour day, starting at 6 a.m. At eight she'd get an eight-minute break; at ten, twenty minutes; at noon, seven minutes.

She described a typical series of repeating assembly actions. 'I had my square metre of the shop floor and I'd operate there for the whole day. The production line would be moving, I'd take a connecting rod, put rings on it, then place a piston on top and block it with a gudgeon pin. After that I'd place the assembled piston in a special basket and it would go to another person who was assembling it with cylinders.' There was leeway for about five seconds either way, for someone else to make up your delay, or for you to make up someone else's. Any more than five seconds and the whole assembly line would stop. Seventy people would be left standing idle. 'There was no time for talking, plus it was super loud in the factory, so we all had earplugs, and could only communicate by nodding heads and with the eyes.' For this, Pasternak took home 1,200 złoty a month (€300) – a 50 per cent increase on her wages in the supermarket. Today, the basic take-home pay for a production line worker in one of Toyota's British plants, where some of these engines were destined, is €1600 a month, and the breaks add up to fifty-five minutes, compared to the thirty-five Pasternak got.

Pasternak got a job at Cadbury's new gum factory in Skarbimierz in 2009, as Mondelez was about to take over. The work was easier than at Toyota – 'I just had to stand there and see everything was working' – and the pay better, the highest of any factory in the area, at 1,500 złoty (€375) a month. In five years, her salary had almost doubled. She got private health insurance, a card entitling her to use private sports facilities, and a free bus on the short ride to work.

One former union official from the gum plant, who asked not to be named, told me that the factory worked well for the first year and a half, when Spanish, French and American managers were running it, but conditions worsened when Polish human resources staff were brought in. Union representation was weak; only one in four workers belonged to a union, and the union officials were inexperienced and poorly supported by their national organisation. Full-time contracts were replaced by temporary contracts; pay was cut. Union officials complained they were subjected to relentless management bullying. In 2011 the union leader at the Mondelez factory, Tomasz Wachowski, was fired for allegedly aggressive behaviour at work. He won his case for unfair dismissal but by that time he'd already moved to the Netherlands. Soon afterwards his deputy was fired, and such power as the union had was broken.

'These multinational companies, they don't just move production to countries that are cheaper, but also to places where workers are easier to manipulate, where there are no strong traditions of worker unions,' Wachowski told me from Holland on Skype. 'We had no previous experience. We got no help from the union. We were like a leaf in the wind.'

An anonymous spokesman for Mondelez in Poland said, by email: 'In general we have a constructive relationship with our labour representatives. We are not aware of any Polish industrial tribunal in this case . . . We do not accept any kind of discrimination, bullying or victimisation.' Pasternak – who wasn't a union member, and spoke of the union in question, Solidarity, as 'totally incompetent' – said she'd been promised, when she started work at Mondelez, that she'd get a full-time contract after fifteen months. Before the fifteen months were up, she was told full-time jobs were no longer on offer; nobody would get more than a two-year contract.

Then the world went off gum. Sales plummeted. There were rumours the plant would be closed completely. Local managers reacted harshly. In 2013, rather than formally announcing that a certain number of people would be laid off, they sought justification for firing people, one by one. 'Basically they fired anyone who'd taken too much sick leave, or talked too much, or expressed dissent,' Pasternak said. 'In my case, it wasn't allowed to bring a mobile phone into the factory, and one day I just had to have my phone with me . . . I just took a look to see whether I'd received a message and I was seen by a supervisor – not even mine! – and because they were looking for reasons to fire people, they fired me.'

Pasternak found another job in a nappy factory built by the Swedish firm SCA in another Wałbrzych sub-zone, in the town of Oława. To get it, she was obliged to be employed not by SCA directly, but by an agency, on a new kind of contract. Formally, the contract was full-time, but in practice, it was only good for a month. Every month she'd get a text message from the agency telling her whether she still had a job or not. In 2015, she found work at the Mondelez chocolate factory, on similar terms. It was a seasonal job, from May till November, packing chocolate bars into Cadbury's 'selection boxes' – Mondelez still uses the Cadbury brand name – for Christmas. For twenty-four hours a day, three shifts of sixty to seventy people worked a 100-metre packing line. Pasternak liked the job and the banter, and in a good month she could earn 2,000 zloty (€500). She didn't get the full-time job she wanted, and the next year, she came back.

This time, Mondelez employed her for the whole season, instead of making her endure the monthly wait to see whether her contract would be extended. But the pay was lower than the year before, and the supervisors made them work harder. They were desperately short-handed, sometimes missing a third of the shift, but they were expected to stuff selection boxes and imitation Christmas stockings with Crunchie bars and Curly Wurlys at a faster rate. 'In chocolate the job was physically exhausting, you had to work hard and fast and the wages were much lower,' Pasternak said. 'People felt they were being treated like garbage. The team leader would come over and yell at us: "You're the worst brigade in the plant! If you can't cope with this, you're the worst!"' Pasternak left before the end of the season and got a job at Donaldson. She's still waiting for a permanent contract.

Mondelez Poland said it employed 'around four hundred people' on 'permanent contracts' and a 'variable' number on temporary contracts. But under Polish law, a 'permanent' contract can actually mean a job that is renewed, or not, every month. Poland leads the EU in temporary contracts, by some margin: 22 per cent of its workforce is on one. Employment agencies in Poland keep coming up with new variants; one agency offered Ukrainian workers with a year's guarantee, like a domestic appliance. 'They recruit in Ukraine and give an employer a warranty – this person will work for one year, and if not, we'll replace them with someone else, equally qualified,' was how Kaśnikowska described it.

Temporary jobs; temporary factories. In 2009 the first multinational to invest in the Wałbrzych zone, the Japanese car parts maker Takata Petri, closed its plant with the loss of 600 jobs and moved production to a special economic zone in Romania, where workers are cheaper. In 1996, in Britain, the Welsh Development Agency agreed a £124 million grant to LG electronics on its promise to invest £1.7 billion and create six thousand jobs. In the end, LG invested much less and ten years later shut down its last assembly lines in Wales, as it ramped up production at its new, subsidised plant outside Wałbrzych. Now LG is sharply cutting jobs at its Polish plant.

Iwo Augustynski was in no doubt that globalisation, unemployment and inequality were behind the success of Law and Justice. The contradictions in their response, he said, were to the party's advantage. 'They don't need to find solutions,' he said. 'It's conflict that gives them power, not solutions.'

I suggested to Maciej Stefanski, the Law and Justice leader and administration head in Brzeg county, which includes the district of Skarbimierz, that it was unwholesome to make so much of his party's concern over the damage globalisation and multiculturalism was doing to Poland, while accepting the iron rules of the free market when the damage was done to the cultural fabric of another country and Poland benefited. But he wasn't buying it; and besides, Mondelez, in its only concession to the fact that it exists in the local space of Brzeg, sponsors the town's Christmas lights. 'Poles really value freedom,' he said. 'This freedom we fought for after 130 years of Polish partition. We don't like it when people from outside try to influence our internal affairs, as the EU does very often. Patriotism is very important to us. It doesn't mean we're against the free markets. We think the special economic zones have enriched Poland.'

Stefanski's office, in another nicely restored prewar building, is cluttered with furniture and knick-knacks. There's a painting of Polish cavalry, another of Józef Piłsudski, who drove the Red Army back from the edge of Warsaw after the Russian Revolution, and a photograph of the town's monument to Pope John Paul II. Images of the same two inspirational figures, by all accounts, adorn the office of the effective leader of Stefanski's party, the former lawyer, former Solidarity activist, former child actor and current conspiracy theorist Jarosław Kaczyński; portals to the psychic hinterland of his movement, a hinterland of Polish Catholicism, martyrdom, suffering, heroism, the battle between good and evil, tattered flags, last stands, saints, miracles, blood, incense, cordite.

Formally Kaczyński holds no office save a seat in parliament. Since his mother died he lives alone, with his cat Fiona, leaving him plenty of time to read Thomas Piketty and Carl Schmitt. He always wears black, in mourning for his twin brother, killed in a plane crash near Smolensk in 2010 that Kaczyński variously blames, without any evidence, on Russia and the then Polish prime minister, Donald Tusk. Everyone assumes the president and prime minister only govern on Jarosław Kaczyński's behalf, that he is the true authority in Poland.

The authority dislikes many things: homosexuals, immigrants, women's reproductive rights, atheists, criticism, dissent. Since coming to power in 2015, the Law and Justice government has taken over public broadcasting, filling it with fawning loyalists and right-wing polemicists on the Russian model. Some 118 journalists have been fired; in one case, six producers and journalists lost their jobs when they refused to prepare a false story smearing the opposition. State TV dropped its annual coverage of Poland's biggest charity event, which raises millions each year for the treatment of sick children, and cut any mention of it from its news programmes, because its organiser also campaigns for the rights of sexual minorities. The government did away with the independence of the chief prosecutor. It tore up the rules intended to ensure senior civil servants are qualified, recruited in open competition, and protected from arbitrary dismissal. The head of the prime minister's office has spoken openly of firing any civil servant suspected of being infected with the 'social pathology' of the previous pro-European, socially liberal, economically centre-right government. The government violated the constitution in order to gain control of the constitutional tribunal, the court that rules on whether laws are constitutional or not. Law and Justice openly encourages emnity towards refugees; just before the election, Kaczyński said they were carriers of cholera and dysentery and 'other, even more severe diseases'. The party backed a bill that would have made abortion absolutely illegal, even in cases of rape, incest or when the mother's life was in danger, and pulled back only after demonstrations. It then passed a law obstructing demonstrations by allowing loyalist groups to reserve potential protest sites indefinitely. It has appointed a militant anti-contraception Catholic theologian to advise on a new sex education course for schools. Senior priests and Law and Justice boost each other. Kaczyński says that 'there are no other moral guideposts in Poland apart from the teachings of the Catholic Church.' In a sermon the arch-bishop of Przemyśl accused opposition MEPs who criticise Law and Justice in the European Parliament of 'fomenting hatred against Poland'.

Even though Brexit threatens Poland with a significant cut to its EU funding, and means difficulties for Poles in the UK, Kaczyński has been energised by it, seeming to believe the shock of Brexit will force Germany and France to give Poland the freedom of action he wants it to have within the

EU. In an interview with the *Frankfurter Allgemeine Zeitung* he portrayed the EU as a creature of Germany, a country in thrall to left-wing ideas, which had pushed Britain towards Brexit as a result of its enforcement of a pro-homosexual ideology. Kaczyński doesn't want to leave the EU: he wants the EU to leave the EU. Whether you call this a bluff, or a calculation that Western Europe has invested too much in Poland not to give it what it wants, Kaczyński is raising the possibility, however remotely, of Poland parting company with the bloc. To be pushed out by an exasperated Germany would be the perfect bloodless modern martyrdom for a modern Poland. But the special economic zones might not look so special afterwards.

Tomasz Wachowski, the sacked union leader at Cadbury's gum factory in Skarbimierz, posted 'well done Britain!' on his Facebook page the day after the Brexit referendum, although he was evasive when I asked him about it. When he lived in Brzeg, he was a founding member of the local branch of the extreme right-wing movement ONR. His sacked deputy was a Law and Justice supporter. Anna Pasternak was hostile; the party's attempts to establish a religious state annoyed her. But nor did she care for Civic Platform, Law and Justice's economically centre-right, socially liberal rivals, who ruled Poland for eight years before Kaczyński's triumph. Like almost half of Polish voters, she sat out the 2015 election. Brexit was won on the votes of more than a third of the electorate; the Conservatives and Donald Trump won power in Britain and the US with the support of a quarter; Law and Justice won it with the support of less than a fifth. The more important question for the Polish opposition is not 'How could they vote for *that*?' but 'Why did they prefer not to vote at all than vote for us?' The populism of Law and Justice is much better known outside Poland than the un-populism of Civic Platform, which raised the pension age, raised VAT – the tax that hits the poor the hardest – and bent over backwards to please foreign investors.

Law and Justice restored the old retirement age and introduced a hefty non-means tested child benefit allowance of 500 złoty a month (€125) for a couple or single parent with a second child, to be funded at least partly by new taxes on foreign investors: not those who built factories – not yet – but those who've come to dominate shopping and retail banking. It also increased the minimum wage. Civic Platform doesn't ask what makes these policies popular: inequality caused by an unfair tax system? Resentment towards foreign supermarkets for the crushing of small Polish shops? A sense that low birth rates threaten Poland's existence? Instead it characterises them as reckless handouts that will destroy the economy. One of the nails in Civic Platform's coffin was a series of transcripts of secret recordings of conversations between government officials published in 2014 in the magazine *Wprost*. Civic Platform, the champion of press freedom, sent in the security services in an unsuccessful attempt to seize the recordings. On one of the tapes a Civic Platform minister, now an EU commissioner, can be heard telling the country's anti-corruption chief that 'only an idiot would work for less than 6,000 złoty a month' – €1,500, twice Poland's average salary.

Barbara Kaśnikowska, the shrewd former head of Wałbrzych zone, suggests, persuasively, that Law and Justice benefited from resentment not of the have-nots towards the haves, but between haves; that as Poland boomed, ordinary people didn't resent those who'd become super-rich so much as people just like them who, for no obvious reason, earned twice or three times as much as they did. In her view, Poland's non-voters didn't despise Civic Platform: they took its achievements for granted. A Pole, on this analysis, is much more likely to vote to say 'screw you' when they are angry than 'thanks!' when all's going well. You can see her point. Andrzej Buła, the marshal of Opole and Civic Platform leader in the province, told me that the EU was funding 40 per cent of the provincial budget, while unemployment had dropped from 14 to 8 per cent. In some counties it's as low as 5 per cent – essentially full employment. Without the Ukrainians, he said, they'd be short-handed. Yet in the 2015 parliamentary elections Civic Platform lost Opole on a swing of 40 per cent to Law and Justice.

There's a word for the work of those who navigate the single field that unites culture and the economy in people's minds: politics. Whatever they are doing, Law and Justice and the English nationalist wing of the Tory Party are doing politics. New Labour, the Tory neoliberal wing and, perhaps, Civic Platform, have drifted into something else. Most shareholder-owned multinationals, away from their home countries, attempted to opt out of culture a long time ago. Instead of forcibly reminding them that they were always part of local culture, whether they wanted to be or not, parties like Civic Platform and New Labour followed business, and began treating economics and culture as two separate things. Out of power, the separation continues, manifesting itself as a split between those waiting for the populists to be destroyed by economic disaster, and those who protest, reactively and sequentially, against each new cultural outrage.

In Britain, seen from the point of view of the workers at Somerdale, the politicians of the first decade of the twenty-first century merged their vision with the governing ethos of multinational corporations like the once paternalistic Cadbury, the ethos of overpaid bosses and the drive for yield on behalf of remote institutional investors. In Poland, Catholic and post-communist culture struggle to interact with the faith-blind, place-blind, history-blind, dreamless giants of global industry.

One of Cadbury's early acquisitions in Poland was Wedel, a chocolate company founded as a family business in Warsaw in the mid-nineteenth century which by the 1930s had grown to be a thriving example of paternalistic capitalism, offering its workforce healthcare, education and housing benefits. The main Wedel factory was destroyed during the Warsaw Uprising. Jan Wedel rebuilt it. The communists nationalised it. The post-communists privatised it. Pepsi bought it. Pepsi sold it to Cadbury. When Skarbimierz was being built, there were fears the strongly unionised Wedel factory would be closed, but it didn't happen, partly because of a campaign to save it, supported by the then mayor of Warsaw, the late Lech Kaczyński, twin brother of Jarosław.* Dariusz Skorek, a union leader at the Wedel plant, told me when I met him in Warsaw that although his union, Solidarity, tended to be described as 'socialist', he was, politically, on the other side.

'The Solidarity movement,' he said, 'is based on Christian values, on right-wing ideology. We were always in opposition

---

*   The EU obliged Mondelez to sell Wedel when it bought Cadbury to avoid Mondelez having a near monopoly on confectionery in Poland. Wedel now belongs to the South Korean firm Lotte.

to the previous government, but Law and Justice – of course they're making a lot of mistakes, but it's a government that's finally started to do something for the workers.

'It's hard for unions in Europe in general, but here, the attitude under the previous government was that they should be destroyed, and there would be no obstacles to foreign investment. I know what people in the rest of Europe are thinking about our current government but from the employee and union point of view, it's *our* government.'

There's an alternative narrative to the Somerdale-as-tragedy story. Cadbury's closure announcement didn't come as a complete shock: workers had noticed that the firm had stopped investing in the building. There were leaks in the roof. Rumours that the factory's days were numbered went back at least as far as 1978, when Dave Silsbury started work. Then, 5,000 people worked there. By 2007, outsourcing and automation had whittled the numbers down to a tenth of that. 'It was almost unthinkable that a machine could wrap an Easter egg, because of the nature of the product and the shape of the egg, but now they can,' Barrie Roberts, a national official from Unite, told me. Because workers in Poland were so much cheaper, automation actually took a step backwards when production moved; the honeycombed sugar in Crunchie bars, which at Somerdale had been automatically cut with high-speed jets of oil, reverted in Poland to being cut the old labour-intensive way with saws. Cadbury could have had a fight on its hands over closure. It had three other factories in Britain, and the national union was ready to support the Somerdale workforce if they chose to strike. But they didn't. Many workers were nearing retirement age, the company's redundancy terms seemed generous, and in the end the majority (not Silsbury or Nicholls) voted seventy to thirty to accept.

After a few tough years, Silsbury and his son found full-time jobs at a local food additives company called TasteTech. Among its customers is the Mondelez chocolate factory in Skarbimierz, part of the £3.8 billion worth of goods Britain exports to Poland every year. In 2017 Silsbury turned fifty-five, and got to access his £100,000 redundancy payment, which he put away in a pension account. 'Keynsham's moved on,' he said. 'I thought there would be a bigger impact than there was. Now it's just as if it was never there.'

Somerdale's best playing fields (the ones that don't flood) have been built over. The architects have made some effort to design the new houses in keeping with the housing built by the company in its Quaker days. But prices are high; it's an easy commute to Bristol. When I visited, the core of the factory itself was being converted into retirement flats. A gigantic sign, designed to be seen from the London to Bristol railway line, advertised the new development's name, the Chocolate Quarter. A sports club was built to replace the demolished Fry Club. In repudiation of its Quaker heritage, it has a bar.

Although the ex-Somerdale workers I spoke to voted Leave, the area as a whole didn't. It's in one of the prosperous Remainer corridors that stretches out from London towards cities of techies, hipsters, students, academics, bankers and cosmopolitan retirees: Cambridge, Brighton, Bristol. Matt Cross, the nearest thing Bristol has to a Maciej Badora – he's director of investment at an agency called Invest Bristol & Bath – told me the UK was at the top of an evolutionary tree of skills, and as low-skilled factory jobs went to cheaper countries, new, high-wage, high-skill jobs were being generated, not necessarily when foreign investors came in, but sometimes, counter-intuitively, when they moved out, releasing highly qualified people into the West Country's ferment of start-ups. A spokesperson for Mondelez, Gemma Pryor, told me the company had increased the number of researchers working on its products in Britain from 25 to 250, intended to keep all its remaining British factories going, and was 'upskilling our wider workforce at Bournville', where £75 million has been invested to keep manufacturing going 'for the next generation'.

True, the optimistic version of the story goes, the EU was wrong to allow Poland to offer Cadbury a subsidy to move. But in the long run, in Europe as a whole, everyone benefits. Eastern Europe gets richer and catches up with Western Europe; instead of 400 million people working and shopping and 100 million people working and queuing, you have 500 million people working and shopping. A bigger market, greater prosperity for all, a peaceful commonwealth, warplanes into chocolate.

The chief of the many flaws in this version is that at both ends of the Somerdale-Skarbimierz journey, the new jobs are worse than the old Somerdale ones. Even supposing all the redundant Somerdale workers, and their children, found similar low-skilled jobs, they would never be as well-paid as they were at Somerdale, and, crucially, wouldn't have the same generous final salary pensions. Some of the Somerdale workers' children, no doubt, will enter the higher-wage higher-skill world of the professional tech class, but the flipside of Matt Cross's optimism is that those jobs will be few, and the zero-hours army many. The outflow of old-style manufacturing jobs, with good pay, conditions and pensions, couldn't be matched by any foreseeable inflow. 'People at the lower end of the workforce,' Cross said, 'start to lose their engagement in the workforce and the jobs they can get are very temporary jobs, minimum wage jobs, the Sports Direct-type model.'

'They weren't our jobs,' Silsbury told me, explaining why, in spite of the good redundancy offer, he'd been ready to fight for Somerdale. 'We were just the keepers of those jobs. We needed to hand them down to our children and our children's children.' Nicholls said he'd been able to retire at fifty-seven and live comfortably, without working, on his Cadbury's pension. He has a caravan in Dorset; he goes fishing; he visits National Trust properties. Shareholder capitalism's race to the bottom means that the generations of non-graduates who come after him – 'there's nothing wrong with someone who hasn't got the ability to be a thinker' – face precarious decades of low-wage warehouse work, followed by poverty on the state pension. Nicholls started out as a trainee chef; now his son is one. But his son is thirty-two. He earns just above the minimum wage and has no Cadbury's to move to. Nicholls's daughter works for the RSPCA. 'She'll never get a big pension, so that's where she'll lose out. She'll always be like she is now, just managing.

'What we had, if you stuck with it, you saw an end game. Now there's no end game. You keep your head above water but the rewards, at the end, don't come through. Once Thatcher started her game and sold off our houses, our kids are in private rented property, and that seems to go up every year, and wages don't. It's going to be a just-managing society. In our generation, the state pension is like a top-up. We are going to have a generation going back to living on the state pension, like the 1930s and 1940s. Do we really want to go back there?'

At Mondelez in Skarbimierz, where casualisation, cost-cutting and fears of being undercut by cheaper labour elsewhere prevail, the target the workers are theoretically aiming for, economic parity with Western Europe, is disappearing from view. The equilibrium, in other words, when the Poles catch up with the Britons, will see a European economy that is, overall, much bigger, but where working-class Britons will have fallen back, and working-class Poles will never enjoy the security and prosperity of their vanished British counterparts in what now seems a mid-twentieth-century golden age. Scaled up to the global level you have a system which, in its search for short-term efficiency and capital yield, restricts the power much of humanity has to consume what it produces. Multinational manufacturers of consumer goods cut their costs to the bone, sweating their wage and pension bill and buying up robots to deliver yield to the pension funds and sovereign wealth funds and hedge funds and wealthy families that own them; but who then will be able to afford the consumer goods? Those people who work for the other guy? But the other guy is doing the same thing. And robots don't eat chocolate.

Afterword

Melanie Onn held Grimsby for Labour at the 2017 election, with an increased share of the vote, while Ukip's support collapsed. In local elections in 2018, Ukip was wiped out, losing all its seats on the council. But its work was done. Onn was swept away in the Conservative landslide of 2019 that secured Boris Johnson's hold on the country, and Britain left the European Union.

The six former blocks of council flats in East Marsh were demolished as planned; wind farm construction offshore proceeds apace. The world's biggest offshore wind farm, Hornsea 1, finished in 2020, is to be maintained from Grimsby, as is its new, larger sister wind farm, Hornsea 2. Much hope is invested in a new plan for the town intended to make Associated British Ports yield a little of its control over the historic Grimsby waterfront, to stimulate the creation of a university franchise in town and, more ambiguously, to create a so-called free-trade zone on the Chinese–Polish model – a marker of Britain's possible transition, post-Brexit, from developed to developing country, undercutting global public services by offering tax and regulation avoidance opportunities to multinationals head-quartered elsewhere. Nearly five years after the Brexit referendum, the future of the British fishing industry remains murky. The same is true of farm subsidies and food tariffs: food, farms and fish, some of the most emotional and powerful rhetorical resources for pro-Brexit politicians, are also the best pawns to sacrifice in the trade games of post-Brexit governments.

In Leicestershire, plans to shrink the number of acute hospital beds have been dropped, but little else about the future is clear. Toby Sanders left for a new job in Northamptonshire. In 2018, in the wake of another terrible winter for the NHS, the government announced it would be increasing the organisation's budget by 3.4 per cent a year in real terms until 2024. The difference between then and now will be an increase of £394 million a week – more than the promised £350 million a week 'Brexit dividend' for the NHS promised by Leavers. In reality, there's no connection between the increase and leaving the EU. Brexit is quite likely to reduce the tax take available for state spending by more than the amount saved through not having to pay for EU membership. And the increase is still less than the amount expert analysts argue the service needs to improve. More immediately, the Covid-19 crisis has thrown the NHS into turmoil. There's evidence that the resource-starved service only coped with the first wave of coronavirus sufferers by sending thousands of frail patients back to their care homes without testing them first. Some of them were infected with Covid and seeded outbreaks up and down the country. The pandemic showed how right the principles of NHS reform supposedly under way are – the need to rebalance the system away from hospitals towards proactive community medicine like testing, towards public health and social care at home for the frail – and also how readily governments can ignore their own policies. Instead of seizing the pandemic moment to bolster local public health teams, create a network of local testing agencies and speed up the reform of social care, the government simply handed over billions to outsourcing companies and consultants to create a hyper-centralised, unresponsive testing regime that doesn't work.

Elections in Poland in 2019 and 2020 kept the populists in power, and there's little sign of the European Union, fighting fires on all fronts, working out how to sanction them. In Keynsham, the local MP, Jacob Rees-Mogg, has become much more famous since I visited the town to write about the chocolate factory. His name came up when Amoree Radford told me about her efforts to save Somerdale in the late 2000s. At that time Rees-Mogg wasn't an MP – Keynsham was represented by Labour – but Radford said Rees-Mogg was more supportive of the campaign than the Labour MP Dan Norris. I never mentioned either of them in the article because it seemed to me Rees-Mogg's 'support' carried no cost for him. But I've often wondered since about the contradiction in that support, especially now that Rees-Mogg is a member of the government. It seems to go to the heart of the Brexit, and indeed the Thatcherite, paradox: how can you be a global free trader, which Rees-Mogg is, and a rampant British nationalist, which Rees-Mogg also is? A little while ago, when I came to write about Rees-Mogg, I asked him about this, and although he answered one of my other questions, he didn't answer that one.

I had to find Rees-Mogg's personal resolution of the Thatcherite contradiction in his public utterances and recordings, which are numerous. And I did. Ultra-low taxes, a starveling state, zero tariffs and zero subsidies are his ideal, but he's quite prepared to depart from it for the sake of political expediency, as long as it's quickie patronage for a client group rather than open-ended, communally funded universal provision as a principle. Short-term tax breaks and giveaways from public funds for client groups whose votes you hope to win, along with a determination to scapegoat minorities and the 'undeserving' poor, is the very essence of populism. So is the assumption that patriotic–cultural spectacles like the launching of aircraft carriers or the birth of royal children will serve as compensation for impoverished lives.

The twist is that while Johnson may be a self-centred cynic, as his enemies portray him, Rees-Mogg genuinely believes in the sacramental character of these spectacles. The Faragist skinny state is unlike the neoliberal skinny state in that it isn't simply about cutting public spending and taxes, but about a polarisation of resources, helping the culturally favoured with shallow buy-outs like Help to Buy or grammar schools. It's about boosting a certain psychogeography of heritage while letting other realms wither: no to the BBC, yes to a new royal yacht. You are defined not by your actions, but by the dreamtime you share. Your living is all Gradgrind; your dream is all Britannia.

London, October 2020

Notes and Acknowledgements

I am, as ever, deeply grateful to the editor of the *London Review of Books*, Mary-Kay Wilmers, and to all those at the LRB who worked on the first versions of the chapters in this book: Alice Attlee, Joanna Biggs, Tom Crewe, Deborah Friedell, Ben Jackson, Tom Jones, Jean McNicol, Paul Myerscough, Joanne O'Leary, Nick Richardson, Daniel Soar and Alice Spawls. I'd also like to thank Natasha Fairweather, Leo Hollis, Matthew Marland, Mark Martin, Maya Osborne and Sarah Shin; Sophy, for her patience and encouragement; and Kay, for making his home with us.

I would like to thank again all those who agreed to be interviewed for this book, and the facilitators of those interviews, particularly Oscar Webb, Paulina Pacuła – my researcher and translator in Poland – Alex Fox, Shaun Knapp, Lee Knifton, Sally Ruane and the Warren family. Wendy Warren died on 27 December 2018. Responding to my account of meeting Louise Warren, her sister Joanne said: 'Louise retrained at age thirty-seven to become a social worker, qualifying when she was forty. She has always special-ised in people struggling with addictions or abusive relationships. Most of us would not want to even start reading about what her clients have faced. She has always been described by her employers and colleagues as strong, compassionate, caring and supportive. She puts herself at risk. She has been a committed Christian since she was fourteen, in a family of atheists, and strongly supported and loved by her fellow church members. I would also say Louise is a realist.'

Deborah Cadbury's book *Chocolate Wars* was a priceless source for the history of the world chocolate industry. Alastair McLellan and Shaun Lintern of the *Health Service Journal* were generous with their time.

Lord Peter Melchett died in August 2018. He was a kind, thoughtful and hospitable host when I met him on his farm, full of hope and gentle enthusiasm and a kind of amazed love for the power of nature and man, working together, to restore a drugged and shackled landscape.

Muriel Barker died in October 2018. She was ninety. Apart from politics, she had a career as a teacher, and Austin Mitchell said of her: 'Her great strength as a teacher and her love of her work was felt by all the children whose lives and minds she'd shaped in school and by the constituents whose interests she'd served as a councillor, but it also influenced and enhanced a strong, sensible, Fabian Grimsby Labour Party.'

In February 2018, Adrian Maximilian Archer, the man I referred to pseudonymously as 'Clem', being cared for on behalf of Leicestershire social services by Lee Knifton, died suddenly of a blood clot. Knifton called him 'a free spirit', and told me his death was 'like losing a child'. Social services declined to contribute towards Adrian's funeral expenses.

London, October 2020